FROM ROME TO SAN MARINO

by the same author

AN ITALIAN DELUSION
A FAMILY FAILING
ASYLUM
BROTHERS AT WAR

From Rome
to San Marino

A walk in the steps of Garibaldi

Oliver Knox

COLLINS
St James's Place, London
1982

William Collins Sons & Co. Ltd
London · Glasgow · Sydney · Auckland
Toronto · Johannesburg

British Library CIP data

Knox, Oliver

From Rome to San Marino: a walk in the steps of Garibaldi
1. Central Italy—Description and travel
I. Title
914.5′6   DG821

First published 1982
© Oliver Knox 1982

ISBN 0 00 216297 0

Photoset in Ehrhardt
Made and Printed in Great Britain by
William Collins Sons & Co. Ltd, Glasgow

For Tim, Peter and Roger

Contents

(dates are Garibaldi's)

ACKNOWLEDGEMENTS

VERY GREAT KINDNESS and hospitality were shown to us by many people during the course of our walk. I think with particular gratitude – in order of our journey – of the proprietor of Al Rivellino of Cetona, Signora Santucci of the Hotel Sobaria at Citerna, Dom Antonio Minciotti of Città di Castello, Professor Franco Fini of Sant'Angelo in Vado; and of the librarians and archivists of Terni, Orvieto, Castiglion Fiorentino, Arezzo, Urbania and Macerata Feltria. Their kindness and that of others too numerous to mention, made the preparation of this book an even greater pleasure than it would otherwise have been.

Nor shall I ever forget several happy mornings spent in the Museo Civico in Bologna, where Signora Gamberini most kindly found me a small desk by the window, and brought me the fascicles of Belluzzi's notes and correspondence.

I must also thank Peter Langdon-Davies and Roger Lubbock, for their companionship on stages of the walk – as well as my son, Tim. Roger may fairly claim to have given me the original idea for the work: he said at a Christmas party, 'I should rather like to do a Garibaldi walk.' It turned out afterwards he had been hoping to make an expedition to Sicily; no matter, the germ was there, and I am most grateful to him.

Finally, I should like to thank my old firm of Sharp's Advertising for their continual support.

SUB-APPENNINES

APPENNINES

San Marino
■ 31
30 ■
Carpegna ·29 ■ Macerata
URBINO ·
S.Angelo in Vado ■ 28
·27 · Mercatello
S.Giustino ■ 26
Cilerna
·24 25
AREZZO ■ ·Città di Castello
22 ■ ·23
Valle
21 ■ · Castiglione Fiorentino
· Cortona
Foiana
20 ■ · Torrita
L. TRASIMENE
Montepulciano
■ 19
· L.CHIUSI PERUGIA·
18 ■ · Sarteano
17 ■ · Cetona
Salci ·
16 ■
Ficulle ■ 15
Prodo
14 13 Todi
·11 12 ·SPOLETO
ORVIETO ·
S. Gemini ·9 10
·Cesi
L. BOLSENA
Terni
■ 8
·Canale della Chiana
·Arno
Metauro
Cesana
Naro
· SIENA
·PESARO

N
W · E
S

· VITERBO
Confine
■7 ·RIETI

Marta

L.VICO
Poggio Mirteto
■6

L.BRACCIANO
■5
Monte Rotondo
■4
· Mentana
3 July
·Tivoli
ROME
Zagarolo

Garibaldi's route..........
Dates of stops ■3 ■ 4 etc

Kilometers
10 20 30 40 50 60

Rome

(1-2 July 1849)

'IS HE YOUR BODYGUARD?'
'Yes indeed. Very good idea to take one to Rome nowadays.
Well, walking all over Italy actually.' There was too much of a
queue behind me to add further information about the footsteps
of Garibaldi.
'I said is he your bodyguard, sir?'
I was with my son at Heathrow. A brief conversation about
bodyguards may have been a little over-solicitous coming from an
airport official, yet did not seem particularly remarkable, the
eleventh victim of kidnapping of the year having that morning been
reported. Perhaps it was something asked nowadays of all
passengers to Italy, when accompanied by younger, tougher men?
Or perhaps it was just a well-worn joke?
Those skyward glances of sons in which embarrassment, pity,
impatience and contempt mingle, are probably familiar to most
fathers, violent kicks on shins rather less usual, and more painful.
'Oh God! Boarding-card, not bodyguard. Boarding-card.
Really.'
But how fortunate I was to have my boarding-card with me, for
the whole month of that long walk, zigzag from Rome up the valley
of the Tiber, westwards across the subapennines into Tuscany,
back eastwards again from the watershed of the Arno into the high
valley of the Upper Tiber, along the route taken by Garibaldi in the
hot days and nights – nights especially – of July 1849, with the tired
remnants of an army, mostly irregulars, which followed him out
into the country after the defeat of the short-lived Roman Republic.
With one cannon, with no base to fall back upon, pursued by the
French conquerors of Rome up to the borders of the Papal States,
and by the Austrians thereafter, this was a march which, for all that
it ended in dissolution and the death of Garibaldi's fierce and

pregnant wife, inspired its first historian Belluzzi the school inspector of Bologna, inspired Trevelyan, continues to inspire students of guerrilla war and of hopeless retreats and of courage in extreme adversity, inspires (I hope) the tale of my own tamer, unharassed walk.

My son had said, 'If you were clever enough to write a film, and make *money*, you would begin with that scene where Garibaldi, dripping with sweat, blood on his red shirt (why didn't it disguise blood?) arrived in the Assembly straight from the battlefield on the Janiculum, his sword too bent for him to sheath it properly, and made his speech about "where we go, there Rome shall be".'

His advice was tinged with scorn. However, I choose to start a little later, at noon on July 2nd, with the short speech Garibaldi delivered in the piazza of St Peter's to his volunteers – and to a sea of Romans, come for the spectacle, as large as may be seen gathered for the coronation or the funeral of a pope. (Then, of course, Rome was popeless, Pius IX having fled in the disguise of an ordinary priest in the previous year, nor would he return from Gaeta, in the Kingdom of Naples, until he had greatly tried the patience of his French restorers.)

'This is all I offer to as many who wish to follow me – hunger, cold, sun. No pay, no barracks, no munitions: but continual raids, forced marches and bayonet fights. He who loves his Country and Glory, let him follow me.'

This may well have been an edited version of the speech, for it could still be picked up in Rome and read, printed on volantini (those scraps of paper which today flutter from cars and strew the streets to advertise political meetings, or gastronomic fairs, or bargain sales) on July 4th, two days after his departure. But the reference to bayonets, lacking in other versions which all give more or less the same sense, rings true: Garibaldi was a great believer in bayonets.

One alternative ending Abba, the Garibaldino chronicler, writing at the turn of the century, believed was deliberately excised from later reports – 'Only the sky for tent, the earth for bed, and God for witness.' Abba thought the mention of God was unwelcome to those who extended Garibaldi's violent hatred of priests (*black cockroaches*) to a disavowal of God. Yet, in his fashion, Garibaldi believed in a deity, possibly regarding him as a kind of celestial *condottiere*: was well-read in the gospels: and retained fragments of that strange blend of Christianity and Socialism, Saint-Simonianism, learnt on one of the long sea voyages of his youth to Constantinople. It was Abba, too, who said that Garibaldi (who was not normally one to take unwarranted risks) was not a fatalist, but did perhaps believe that he was Fate itself.

To this speech, spoken astride his great white horse, Garibaldi added that all those who wished to follow him on his uncharted march should meet him in the square of St John of the Lateran, at six o'clock that evening. This is about twenty minutes' walk from the modern railway terminus and some four miles from St Peter's. In the sidestreets not far from here, on the evening before our own departure from Rome, I did something which I doubt Garibaldi would ever have done with so little forethought: enter a casual barber's shop to have my hair cut for the long walk. For he was immensely vain of his long, flowing hair, keeping it beautifully clean and combed, so much so that he liked to compare himself, and to hear himself compared, to a lion: a simile he uses more than once in his long, and not wholly indifferent, autobiographical poem.* Referring to his retreat from Rome and to himself as a lion, he wrote:

> The lion who's pressed upon
> By hordes of jackals sometimes halts – and turns
> So that the craven mob upon his heels
> Shrinks back in fright to see him unafraid.

The barber was round the corner from a café Garibaldi. Throughout Italy cafés, statues, streets, hotels, even restaurants (although Garibaldi was a frugal eater), bear witness to the sad truth hit upon by Max Beerbohm, writing a half-century or so later,

'In St James's Street, has anyone ever fancied he saw the ghost of a pilgrim wrapped in a cloak, leaning on a staff? Other ghosts are there in plenty. The phantom chariot of Lord Petersham dashes down the slope nightly. Nightly Mr Ball Hughes appears in the bow window of Whites. At cockcrow Charles James Fox still emerges from Brooks's. Such men as these were indigenous to the street. Nothing will ever lay their ghosts there. But the ghost of St James, what should it do in that gallery? Of all the streets that have been

* See Appendix 2.

named after famous men, I have but one whose namesake is suggested by it. In Regent Street you do sometimes think of the Regent; and that is not because the street is named after him but because it was conceived by him . . .'

Yet my barber, being so very near the café Garibaldi, at least gave me an easy opening. 'Actually, I'm following the footsteps of Garibaldi from Rome to San Marino in the summer of 1849 – on foot.'

'In a car,' corrected the barber.

'No. On foot. All the way to San Marino. The republic.'

The barber poised his clippers motionless over my head, and stared long seconds at his own reflection in the looking-glass. Possibly he thought he was the victim of some practical joke, was cutting the hair of a lunatic. He humoured me. 'Bravo,' he said, smiling not believing.

'I shall take about a month.'

'Tivoli, Terni, Todi, Orvieto, Arezzo, over the mountains . . .' He had recovered and, a little playfully, was waving his cut-throat at me.

This was an impressive and entirely accurate recital of towns on the route. Later I was to learn that the Garibaldi Retreat formed part of the primary education of most Italians of his age, equivalent of our own King Alfred burning the cakes, our own Charles II hiding in an oak tree near Worcester. It was worth asking what else he knew.

'How many people went with him on the march? Only one with *me*.'

'A thousand.'

Confusion with the *mille* who sailed from Genoa to conquer Sicily and Naples some ten years later? But the barber may be forgiven. No one at the time knew how many men did follow him when the signal was given to depart at eight o'clock on the evening of July 2nd.

The *Morning Chronicle*'s own correspondent put it at 2–3000. The *Observer* reported that Garibaldi with 3–4000 men was believed to have taken the road to Albano. The British consular agent reported that he took with him an army of 4000. The French newspaper *Moniteur* in its official column of July 7th, spoke of 5–6000 men heading in the direction of Torrecini. The London *Times* estimated there were 4000 infantry and 500 horse, adding:

'The partisans' own battalion did not amount to more than 800 men, but as he announced his intention not to lay down his arms and invited all those inclined to follow him to inscribe their names, all the desperate men who were left alive from the work of slaughter which fell so heavily on his comrades joined him, and full of confidence in his star started in the direction of the Abruzzi.'

And by the time the news had crossed the Atlantic Garibaldi's army had swollen to 10,000 men, reported by the *New York Tribune* to be heading towards the Neapolitan frontier.

The wildly inaccurate intelligence of the press and of his pursuers was largely due to his own deliberate deception; and it greatly assisted him.

Standing beneath the great colonnaded façade of St John Lateran, the 'cathedral of Rome and therefore of the world', it is easy in the mind's eye to fill the very large piazza with 4000 men or more, to recreate the scene on that hot, still, July evening.

But it is high time to introduce my other constant companion of the walk, a paper companion this time, Major Hoffstetter, late of the Swiss army, and staff officer of Garibaldi throughout the siege and the Retreat. Slight, dapper, moustached, looking exactly as I would expect a Swiss Major to look, his portrait hangs just above Garibaldi's in the room dedicated to the General in the Museum of San Marino. On the back of the photocopied pages of his account, written in German and translated by himself into idiosyncratic Italian, I made my own scribbled notes. What an admirable man he was! Among his amiable qualities was a liking for the different wines of the towns through which they passed, an eye even during the most fatiguing hours of the march – after midnight, say, under a full moon on top of a high pass in the Apennines – for the spectacular view: an eye, too, even if ascribed to the men under his command, for the occasional pretty girl.

His is the best and fullest of the three eye-witness accounts of the march. Trevelyan in his notes refers to him as Hoff, and I fell myself into the habit of thus abbreviating him.

Since, for all my proud talk to the barber, we had no intention ourselves of walking through the desolate suburbs of Rome – dereliction of duty though that might be – but meant instead to catch an early morning train to Zagarolo, some twenty-five kilometres south-east, in order to 'rejoin' Garibaldi at the point where he switched direction and headed northwards up steep

15

valleys, the first leg of that night's journey must be all Hoffstetter's. He writes of the pain in his heart at the departure when many of those who had promised to come failed to show up, when the crack regiment of the Bersaglieri, and the National Guard, did arrive, but only to salute the General and not to join him (save for a few): his sorrow at reining in his horse many times, and looking back at 'the towers and palaces of the eternal city' as he covered the retreat.

'The march continued without any pause and in the utmost silence from ten in the evening until seven o'clock the next morning. No one could smoke, orders were given in hushed tones. The General marched in this hidden, hurried way because he wanted to gain time, and reach the mountains quickly. Some patrols on horse flanked his right wing, and the vanguard bit by bit trotted till they were several miles ahead.'

No one smoked! To the liberal revolutionaries, the smoking of cigars was one of the badges of their creed.

Hoffstetter recites the order of the march, too, given to him by Garibaldi in a house close to the gate of St John just before nightfall.

> Garibaldi and his wife Anita + 50 horse
>
> 800 paces
>
> Company of infantry
>
> Baggage train – mules, donkeys, two-wheeled carts and a couple of carriages for the wounded
>
> Cavalry with the one and only cannon
>
> Infantry, with one cohort for rearguard
>
> Bersaglieri and Finanzieri with 20 horse, of whom 10 lie 800 paces back, to form the last patrol

The Bersaglieri, founded by King Charles of Piedmont in 1821, were, still are, crack troops accustomed to running at the double both in ceremonies and in action. Finanzieri are more difficult to explain. The English do not expect their customs officers and tax inspectors to be a particularly romantic or military section of Her Majesty's service. But still today in Italy that section of the police known as the Guardia Finanziere run the most colourful advertising for recruits: customs launches throw up white bow-waves in pursuit of drug- and cigarette-laden yachts: skiers swoop down through pine forests after jewel and currency smugglers on the Swiss borders.

But where was this long, silent column heading?

In the immediate future, the answer is a crab. That is to say, as with nearly all his marches this month, Garibaldi took two sides of the triangle in order to reach his destination. He seldom left a camp, or a city in his true direction. That was clearly intended to mislead. And the ruse was successful, however frustrating it must have been for those who followed him to find themselves, in dead of night, after hours of marching, leaving a straight road to climb at right angles up a steep mule-path, hauling after them carts and the solitary cannon.

According to Hoffstetter, he told nobody where he was going on each stage: and he deliberately kept people guessing about his larger aims, or ultimate destination. For example, in his autobiography he says that he hoped to put up a good fight – *fare una bella guerra* – in the mountains. But at the time he told the Minister of War that he meant to cross the Apennines, reach the Adriatic and go to the aid of besieged Venice. Some people understood that he meant to set up a Republican Government-in-exile in Spoleto – which the Austrians hadn't yet reached. Later on there was his proclamation in Montepulciano, where he hoped, however briefly, to raise Tuscany to his side.

We argued about the seeming inconstancy of his ambition on the evening before we set out. What exactly was Garibaldi up to, how often did he change his mind, what was the ultimate goal he had set his heart on? My own belief is that he never himself knew, but juggled all the balls in the air all the time. And maybe the successful guerrilla leader commits himself as little as possible, whether to himself or to others.

And the motives of his enemies? There is an ambiguity about those of the French which has a familiar ring. They had intervened, they said in effect, in order to forestall. Their cabinet had declared that the occupation of Rome was undertaken, (i) in order to watch other powers who sent armies into the Italian states and (ii) to guarantee the liberal institutions granted by the Pope before his flight to Gaeta.

These institutions, the French maintained, would be in jeopardy he were to be restored, without conditions, by the reactionary Austrians. Thus they were able to square the circle, at least to their own satisfaction, and remain at once the Father of Revolution and the Eldest Daughter of the Church.

General Oudinot for the time being had achieved enough with his victorious entry into Rome, to satisfy Catholic sentiment in France. No need to upset the Republicans at home still further by coming to bloody grips with Garibaldi, for all that '600 convicts to whom he gave liberty formed part of his corps' (*Sentinelle*, Toulon 11/9) or 'Garibaldi and his adventurers have taken with them many precious articles' (*Moniteur* 11/9).

Enough to see the desperadoes out of the territory of the Papal States. Let Garibaldi be a bother to others.

As some English saw it too. The *Manchester Guardian* on July 21st wrote: '. . . if it were not so manifestly in the interests of the French to get rid of him it might be supposed that General Oudinot had permitted Garibaldi to escape to be a thorn in the side of the Neapolitans and prevent their interfering in the Papal States.'

And the *Illustrated London News*, whose reports and illustrations gave the English the fullest picture of life in Rome, and of the exotic band of Garibaldini, ostrich feathers in their hats, wrote: '. . . a detachment of Oudinot's army was ordered after him . . . much it is supposed for the look of the thing and with no serious intention of capturing him.'

So, though he was not to know it, his principal enemy in the immediate future was something of a paper tiger.

These were some of the papers I re-read in our hotel room the night before taking the suburban train to Zagarolo.

❦ II ❧

Tivoli

(3 July)

E NCUMBERED WITH NEW PLASTIC RUCKSACKS overfull with heavy-duty woollen socks, wearing new alpine walking-boots which squeaked and chafed the ankles, two Englishmen, one old, one young, stumbled past the street cleaners and the grey litter of grandly-named *pensiones* – Ascot, Eton, where is the Ritz, there is a Ritz near *Paddington?* – at 0645 on a chill March morning in 1980, just under 100 years after the death of the guerrilla in whose footsteps they were following.

If anyone else is tempted to follow in the same footsteps, they will do well to reconnoitre Rome station the day before. For the line to Zagarolo starts at the far end of an endlessly long side platform: is indeed a line of a different order, of a different gauge even, from those worn down by the great trains which travel north and south: was one of the very few to be constructed in the Papal States before the Unification, taking passengers in wooden carriages towards the borders of the Kingdom of Naples.

The flat Campagna at dawn, with its scraps of ruined aqueducts, its fallen columns, much of it covered in asphodel and tall rush-grasses, can still, despite its modern debris of wrecked cars and broken-windowed factories, easily be imagined as the deserted, malaria-infested plain that it was at the time of the Retreat.

At nine o'clock, Time deserving its old-fashioned notation now that Rome had been left behind and the train very late, we stopped at Zagarolo station, or rather at the halt for the small hilltop city which lies twenty minutes' walk away: the only two passengers to alight on the crumbling cement of the platform. No coffee, an overcast morning, and the shutters of the windows of the deserted ticket office flapped and banged.

'Ugh! Madness! Especially as you don't even *know* Garibaldi came this way. Do you?'

19

'The whole point . . . But I won't argue.'

I didn't like to confess that we were taking the word of one old man, speaking to Belluzzi the school inspector of Bologna decades later who wrote: 'A fine man, he had followed Garibaldi up to the point till he passed his own home. His name was Bernadino Melchiorre or Melchiorre Bernadini. Twice, once at Terni and once in Acquasparta, he told me of this halt and it is this which may make one suppose that Garibaldi left Rome by Via Casilina and not Tiburtina (which would have been the direct way to Tivoli).' Frail evidence!

After breasting one small rise, the road towards Palestrina dips and there at the bottom of the deep hollow one fork of the road points left towards the brick-red city, built on a spur above two clefts running more or less due north and south. Along either of these Garibaldi might have marched, avoiding the city itself so that – though surely the noise of the clanking of the bridles would have carried up the hill? – the inhabitants could easily have preferred, or pretended, to have heard nothing in the small hours of that dark night. Zagarolo itself, approached up a long chestnut-lined avenue, records no memory of his passage; for one can scarcely count the broad Corso Garibaldi by which we entered, to reach, in the centre, a fountain formed from a vast antique bath-tub.

Breakfast of cappuccinis and rolls, in a café where already the Space-Invader machines were being worked with relentless and passionate concentration by the young boys of the town. This, our first halt, seemed a good time to spare a thought for Anita, the General's Brazilian wife who for all her tirelessness, her insistence that she should accompany her husband whatever the perils, must surely, in the sixth or seventh month of her fourth pregnancy, have welcomed a brief rest even more than most. She was last seen leaving Rome '. . . dressed in a legionnaire's blouse – though longer than usual – with men's trousers tucked into high boots of polished leather. Across her shoulders she wore a tricolour sash, on her head a soft hat with an ostrich feather in it: she was armed with sabre and pistol and mounted on a fine piebald . . . two boys from Bologna, riding Corsican ponies, acted as her pages.'

How I should like to know what this spirited and obstinate lady thought of the others who were riding up front of the column, jostling around Garibaldi himself! The Barnabite priest, for example, Ugo Bassi – did she really manage to control, in his

Tivoli (3 July)

favour, the loathing she had for priests, more virulent even than that of her husband? True, he was held very dear by Garibaldi, who, Bassi wrote, used to say '. . . it was by the inspiration of God I had come to be with him, I must be the Love that binds the soldiers to the people – "The People" Garibaldi says, speaking always like an angel, "in whom only lies my force, in whom only is my supreme hope."' *Vox populi, vox dei!* True, too, that the priest was wearing the regulation red shirt, though partially concealed by a very long grey beard. Yet he was nevertheless also wearing a wide-brimmed French priest's hat, a large crucifix on a silver chain hung round his neck, and in the purse of his bandolier he carried the unfinished manuscript of his only work *La Croce Vincitrice* – suitably militant title – a phial of holy oil, and a breviary. Mounted on a splendid sorrel (said 'once to have belonged to the English Ambassador'[*sic*]) he must, even in the darkness, have been an unmistakable companion.

'Try to quote. Bet you can't.'

'Er . . .'

How agreeable to self-esteem had I been able to quote melodious, appropriate lines as we resumed our pilgrimage after breakfast! Fortunately for my companion this is not a gift with which I am endowed.

The valley down into which we now zigzagged is called by the curious name 'Fosso di valle inversa', and it did indeed give us the impression that we were walking uphill through that sultry pre-noon, rather than slowly, very slowly, descending towards the Aniene, tributary of the Tiber. The optical illusion may have been due to the valley narrowing, and its wooded sides becoming steeper as we approached the turreted Castello del Passerano – just as though we were indeed climbing upstream, towards a strongpoint. Perfect ambush country! Easy to imagine French cavalry reining in at the top of the defile, and the long column trapped. That may well have been Garibaldi's fear as he hastened towards the mountains, even although he was still under cover of darkness as he pressed his army along, riding up and down, in hushed tones exhorting his officers.

What an extraordinary speed he made! It was something his enemies could never get used to. To have left the gates of Rome at eight o'clock and arrived at Tivoli, nearly fifty kilometres distant by this route, by seven the next morning! And this was the main body,

21

for an advance guard of the cavalry rode ahead. Our respect for the infantry, our understanding of the need for copious requisitions of boots at every stopping-place, grew as we ourselves trudged on, train-cheaters though we had been. Two hours of walking had taken us exactly ten kilometres on, and midday was approaching.

'Surely somewhere underneath that castle, don't you think? An ancient hostelry of some kind, used by grooms. Serving-wenches and so on?'

'Too early in the morning for *that*.'

Seignorial woods ran down right to the edge of the road. There was an air of eighteenth-century parkland, a smell of civilization. A cluster of outhouses, stables, gave further encouragement. The banks of the streamlet running through the wood were well tended. From the battlements a hundred feet or so above us I thought I could make out two figures, observing us. Round the corner, nestling into the hillside, there must be at least a café. And we were in Frascati country!

But there was no café.

Only white boulders, by the edge of the road, which stretched straight, long and empty before us. Later, one or two small vineyards, with skew wooden boards announcing that they were for sale, seemed also to mock our thirst.

'What time of the morning would it have been for the General?'

'We're still about two hours from Tivoli. Say five o'clock.'

If at breakfast I had thought, with pity, of Anita, it was now the time to invoke, with reservations, the shade of Ciceruacchio, the wine merchant. That may not be quite the right term. He was a self-made pothouse-keeper, a genial, generous rabble-rouser from the slums of Rome. Belluzzi says 'a large man astride a small horse, he was a most unmilitary figure'. He had done much to bring Rome to tumult and revolution. Only six months earlier he had been the organizer of festivities when cardinals' hats had been taken from the shop windows of hatters and thrown into the Tiber: and the mob, chanting the De Profundis, had consigned the Pope's New Year appeal from Gaeta, to the public lavatories.

Two of his sons accompanied him. One, in front of the column with the General and himself, was only thirteen years old. The other was the youth almost certainly responsible for knifing in the neck Pellegrino Rossi, the Pope's moderate Prime Minister. This murder, vaunted by Garibaldi to the end of his life, led proximately to the setting-up of the Republic, and deserves more, far more, than the tut-tut of liberal historians. It casts an indelible slur on the whole chapter. But the rogue would at least have known now where to find drink. The motorway eastwards to Pescara ran at right angles across our thirsty path. From this Adriatic port, it was thought at the time, Garibaldi might have embarked his men on fishing boats to Venice, having slipped in between the armies of Naples and those of Austria (marching south from Ancona).

Underneath the motorway pillars, and out on the other side, we looked in vain for any sign of refreshment. The skies lowered and a very few, very heavy drops of rain splashed noisily on our rucksacks. Gloomily above us the dark villas and churches of Tivoli, built into the mountainside, were now revealed, now hidden, in swirling thunderclouds. And then, at the junction with the Via Tiburtina, the miracle! One of those sprawling new cement restaurants, unfrequented save on Saturday nights and Sunday lunchtime, neon-signed, quite commonly to be found a few kilometres outside provincial towns. *AL CACCIATORE. Tagliatelle Casalinga. Pollo ai cipolli. Fettucine al cacciatore.* The smell of mushrooms, the taste of fruity but dry Frascati! The pleasure of satisfied greed, reinforced by the sight, outside the drenched windows, of a *bus stop*, opposite! For the skies were staging a deluge, as they know so well how to do in Italy, the universe being remorselessly blotted out in 'whole sheets of sluicy rain'. We would be let off the last half-hour limping up to Tivoli: we would take the bus.

'How on earth did he get five thousand people to follow him, I'd like to know? They can't *all* have been criminals.'

'Oh, he was said to have a low, soft, musical voice. Compelling eyes. That sort of thing. Of course, some *were* criminals whom he pardoned. Like Ciceruacchio's son.'

Others, whether compromised or not, fled from the French occupiers of Rome by other means. The British consular agent Freeborn took it upon himself to issue a great number of passports, for which he was at first rebuked by Palmerston. Many of them made their way to Malta, giving rise to the heartfelt plea from the Bishop of that island, echoed, in less frank terms, by so many unwilling hosts of refugees before and since.

'May the Lord will that they may, in any other land, distant from this, live and amend their lives.'

This was a moment when to us, footsore, the journey to Malta seemed less arduous than our own prospective march to San Marino. But how well-fed we were!

Had we known what was awaiting us in Tivoli we might not have been quite so discursive and satisfied over our lunch. Alighting from the bus on the broad expanse of the Largo Garibaldi (in and around which the General pitched camp in the cool shade of trees) we skeltered beneath the continuing deluge to the nearest bar. I asked,

'And can you recommend a small hotel?'

'There are no hotels in Tivoli. One ten kilometres towards Rome.'

'Two beds, one bed. Anything.'

'Nowhere to sleep in Tivoli at all.'

Tivoli, city of waterfalls, fountains, great villas and gardens, has been a fashionable resort since 90 BC, and has over 20,000 inhabitants. We put on our plastic mackintoshes and ran to the next bar. Did we look too disreputable? For again, there was not a hotel, not a single room. We said to each other,

'This is a far cry from the reception Garibaldi got. Hoffstetter speaks of cheering crowds coming out to meet them. Lots of food and wine.'

'And lots of fresh water. At least there's that.'

'Let's stay in the bar and wear them down.'

After several more drinks I returned to the attack. I said to the barman,

'I am an English historian. We are following in the footsteps of Garibaldi in July of 1849 etc. etc., we have walked from Rome and we must find beds for the night.'

'Walked? On foot?' He looked at me strangely.

'And we are very tired.'

He sighed and shrugged. Reluctantly he scribbled something.

'You might try this number. It's called Eden e Sirene.'

The Eden e Sirene, with its tiled verandah overlooking a waterfall that leaps from crag to crag into a deep green pool, its faded wicker chairs, some of them with four legs, its whitewashed bedrooms for less than £4 a night, welcomed us (when at last someone answered a bell) as the hotel's only guests: and its only happy guests we remained save for one harassed Italian lady, descending from a taxi in the downpour, equally flummoxed to find no one except ourselves, whom at first she took to be the proprietors.

Why such reluctance in the town to give us the name of this establishment, named so aptly after the lost Paradise, and the alluring Sirens? Possibly it was due to some local feud, or political warring. For conflict in the spring of 1980 was bitter in Tivoli. The MSI, party of the extreme right, held the uneasy balance of municipal power.

Rusty guns hung, not very securely, on the walls of the restaurant. They wobbled when I touched them.

'Flintlocks.'

'Garibaldian, do you think?'

'These are earlier. Hoffstetter says that all two thousand five hundred of the infantry were armed with percussion guns. And carried fifty cartridges each in their cartridge belts.'

Percussion guns were a fairly recent development. By the 'fifties they used copper caps, first developed by a certain Joseph Egg in England in 1823, which were filled with mercury fulminate; and they were a great advance on flintlocks – much more reliable, quicker to load and fire.

'I'm glad I didn't have to help haul that cannon. Of course, there was an old type of cannon called a Siren, too . . .'

Hoffstetter, in describing the state of the expedition's armament in Tivoli, writes engagingly, 'Our total artillery was just one cannon . . . drawn by four horses. Very useful if any city should choose to defy us. A couple of shots would have been quite enough to *terrify*. Besides, it led the enemy to believe that we had artillery with us.'

The review and reorganization of his armaments and men was the business which occupied Garibaldi during the daylight hours of July 3rd. He had a liking for Roman nomenclature, being powerfully affected by the legends of the glorious past of Rome. This casts a long shadow forward to that other *Duce*. Hence he divided the first of his two legions (regiments) into three cohorts (battalions) each of which was again divided into six centuries (companies). Each century, as its name implies, consisted of about 100 men.

The 400 cavalry were at first led by one Italian and one Polish Major and later put under the command of the vain and testy South American Colonel Bueno. He was an old companion in arms of Garibaldi in Montevideo: he had carried his General, immobilized by rheumatism, on his shoulders into the first Assembly of the Roman Republic; and his desertion towards the end of the Retreat – probably with the money-chest – greatly grieved Garibaldi.

The cavalry's tackle was poor; as a force it could not be considered battleworthy. But how precious it was for reconnaissance, for feints and ruses; for riding to cities ahead to drum up provisions, to encourage (or enforce) welcome!

Amid these military preoccupations, it is agreeable to find Hoffstetter, who was made Second-in-command of the Staff, alive to the civilized delights around him. He writes, 'Tivoli is surrounded by woods – the sacred groves of antiquity – and lies on a mountain set apart from others, a city of far-famed and enchanting waterfalls. In amongst green fragrance and gardens of pleasure, arise its venerable temples and ruins.'

Two of these temples, that of the Sibyl and of the Vestal Virgins, we visited after dinner, reaching them within a couple of minutes through the door of the restaurant. Standing within the circle of fluted Ionic columns, carved from local travertine stone, we could smell the wet Roman pines above, hear the splash and echo of the tumbling waters below.

'Tomorrow we must see the Garibaldi statue, read his memorial plaque, visit the archives in the Villa d'Este. Even do some non-Garibaldi sightseeing.'

'Anything rather than a five-hour walk in the rain.' For it was still pouring.

The plaque in the Largo Garibaldi, duly inspected, translates as follows,

In this place,
The hero Garibaldi
the terror of his foes
the idol of the people
stayed awhile with his warriors
on the third of July 1849,
when, overpowered but untamed
by two great armies,
he kept safe for his Country that right arm
which, fighting loyally by the King's side,
made Italy One and Free.

Who would guess from this inscription how glad the city was to see him leave its gates: how not a single volunteer was to offer to join his ranks, already depleted during the night's march: how his hope of fermenting a revolution of the People in the country here received its first dowsing? For, as he must bitterly have come to realize during the next month, the chief concern of the cities through or near which he passed, was so to judge the warmth of this welcome and the generosity of their supplies as not to incur the penalty of even larger, forced 'contributions': in short, how to see him on his way at the least possible cost to the community.

But this is to run ahead a little. The citizens of Tivoli would have learnt only the day before of the fall of the capital into the hands of the French. They would doubtless have been told – by the outriders of the General if by no one else – that Garibaldi had, as one of the last acts of the dying Assembly, been given plenipotentiary powers, so that he could now be considered, as he certainly considered himself, the very embodiment of Rome-in-Exile. 'Where I go, there Rome shall be.' Prudent though their welcome might have been, prudent their unwillingness to join his army, they may well have been saluting the brave defenders of the Republic with genuine enthusiasm. It was only later in the Retreat that the approach of the 'Banda Garibaldi' was viewed with so much dread and alarm by the municipal authorities (and, I suspect, by most of the inhabitants, too).

'Do you detect a touch of sarcasm in that line about his later "fighting loyally by the King's side"?'

'You may say sarcasm. I think self-deception. I'm kinder than you are.'

After the final unification of Italy in 1870, it was usual for Garibaldi's Republican past to be pushed back discreetly into the shade, his later services to King Victor Emmanuel II to be brought forward into the light – a weatherhouse of a reputation. Arguable, too, that loyalty to the titular unifier of Italy was easy to reconcile with earlier, passionate hostility towards the temporal sovereignty of the Pope: with the pure milk of Roman Republicanism, that is.

Poor Pius IX! So bitterly blamed for his lagging behind other Italian states in martial eagerness to rid the country of its Austrian oppressors that he was, in effect, dethroned! Yet can anyone today seriously believe that the Prince of Peace, the spiritual sovereign of so many millions throughout the world, should be blamed for his refusal to declare war, his unwillingness, as Farini put it, to be 'a Pontiff on the white mule at the head of the new Crusaders'?

That, of course, was the decision that had led swiftly to Mazzini's hour of Republican glory, to French intervention, to Garibaldi's defence, defeat and Retreat.

❦ III ❦
Monterotondo
(3-5 July)

'HOFF SAYS QUITE CLEARLY that when Garibaldi left Tivoli he walked south for an hour and a half, then suddenly turned right, across fields, until he found somewhere to camp at midnight near a spring. And very near Tivoli.'

'How on earth can you look for a tiny spring in this rain? The best bet is Monticelio.'

Agreement was reached by the time we had walked, or rather waded, to the Tivoli bus station. The tiny town of Monticelio perches on and around the top of another of the olive-clad hills which arise from the Campagna to form a distant ring round Rome. The bus wound past the travertine quarries and the sulphur baths, taking almost an hour on the journey, but since Monticelio lies only eight kilometres as the crow flies north-west from Tivoli, I suppose that by Garibaldian marching standards it might be accounted as 'very near'. We ourselves arrived at about ten in the morning, determined now, on the next stage, to brave any weather.

A small streamlet does arise just west of the church of Santa Maria. Honour would have to be satisfied with that. In the bus stop café nearby, the card-players stopped, some of them turned their chairs full circle to stare at us. One of the older pensioners took his pipe out of his mouth. But he was so courteous, took such pains in directing us on to the best path to St Angelo that he was spared my speech, already growing fluent, about being an English historian following in the footsteps of . . . etc. etc.

Soon we were walking downhill towards the saddle which separates the twin eminences of Monticelio and St Angelo, passing olives the undersides of whose leaves were far brighter than the covered sky. The sides of our gravel road, marked only as a mule-track on the 1:100,000 map, seemed about to slither downhill, landslides imminent before our eyes. A typical dilemma then approached us – whether to go up a narrow valley by an ill-defined path (which was the most direct way) or to follow the gentler and more circuitous road. Church bells rang out above us.

'You saw in the archives that notice of the Republican triumvirs demanding church bells be converted into cannons?'

'You take the high road.'

'I prefer the low road.'

'We will meet at the bar nearest the Duomo.'

I recommend this method of assignation in Italy, since there is always a Duomo, always a bar. Having said that I must record our only failure.

Panting up a steep, muddy cattle-path, gasping at the cemetery gates on the outskirts of the town, I reached at last the steps of the church whose bells I think were those we had heard an hour earlier. Asking whether this was the Duomo (or principal church), whether that the nearest bar, how reassured I was by the sight of two small Fiats, delivering elm logs to what was – evidently – more than just a bar. Wood smoke aroused hopes of lunch.

Small puddles formed in the corner where I laid down my rucksack, ordered wine and waited. How to fill in the triumphant interval before my son rejoined me? Surely, by rescuing a few soggy photocopies of Hoffstetter pages from my anorak pocket, and reconsidering the General's route along these broken foothills of the Lucretilan mountains.

Some of the tracks, so the local peasants told him, were impassable to carts. He was undeterred. Already he was beginning to dispense with wheeled transport. Eight mules had been requisitioned in Tivoli. Sick and wounded would have to forgo the comfort of a jolting wagon.

The main body had started two hours late from their midnight bivouac – at four o'clock – and had marched, as was to become their custom, until ten, when the vanguard reached Monterotondo. That was their morning exercise. Six hours could mean (my map measurer wobbled over the café table) anything up to thirty kilometres, although, however near Tivoli Garibaldi had encamped it seems that, having executed his great feint towards the Neapolitan borders, he may not have felt the need to press on quite so quickly as before. Who could possibly have guessed that he was circling around Rome, rather than away from Rome, and was now heading *west*?

And their food? Neither that day nor any other was there a shortage of meat and wine; the meat roasted on spits and eaten bare of fat, without salt. 'Those American Roasts were delicious,' says Hoffstetter, adding that this un-Italian diet aided them greatly in their extraordinary exertions. But often there was no fresh bread, and most of the soldiers, not having rucksacks or suitable pockets, carried loaves, threaded on a cord, round their necks.

The time needed for contemplating Garibaldian food and drink, and speculating about my own, seemed to have been more than long enough for my fellow-traveller to have rejoined me, however slow and serpentine the road he had foolishly chosen. Bedraggled, irate, he burst in just before three o'clock.

'What on earth do you mean, *you* won? *I* won. I've been sitting hours in the café nearest the church.'

'But *this* is the principal church. That one, the one you can see from here.'

Ah for *campanilisimo*! Even in a city of a few hundred souls, there can be found, at one end of the town, citizens who will sturdily refuse to acknowledge the existence, let alone the superior status, of a church at the other end.

In the face of lunch, further recrimination faded. On the stroke of three o'clock a birthday party of twelve guests arrived, stamped the rain from their shoes, and filed into the small, dark back room to which we were then summoned, and shown the only other rickety table. Impossible to hope for more succulent tagliatelle, more generous slices of veal, grilled on the embers of the elm logs I had helped to carry in! Two hours later, after having shared in the toasts, and the birthday cake, we staggered out underneath clouds that were now only spitting; and walked, mercifully downhill, through narrow streets made bright with window-boxes, towards the fitful western sky.

'Not too late in the least. Garibaldi didn't begin *his* second marches till the evening.'

'He was younger than me.'

'And thinner.'

'It will be dark by the time we reach Monterotondo.'

For ours was a ragged spring day, dusk not far off, eight miles still to walk. And then an extraordinary boon was granted us. At a bend in the asphalt road, a leafy path branched off, in a better direction. This path opened out into a meadow, set in a valley about

200 yards wide, with a small stream – the original running brook of the Forest of Arden – which flowed sweetly down its centre, between occasional patches of watercress. A gentle, downhill, twilight walk! On either side of the stream the turf was close-cropped by sheep. The prospect was bounded to north and south by woods of old beech trees, their buds showing the first haze of green. To crown this idyllic and pastoral scene, worthy of an eighteenth-century English watercolourist, we saw approaching us a vast flock of sheep, so thick that it almost filled the valley. As they approached I heard the shepherd whistle, though I could not tell the tune, and the first shaft of sunlight seen since Rome touched their fleeces as they jostled and tinkled towards us.

When they surrounded us, it was as though we were half-submerged in a sea of white foam, swimming or wading against the current.

'Garibaldi, if you remember, drove his meat with him on the hoof, just as he had done fighting on the prairies of Uruguay.'

'His beef, not his mutton. You couldn't drive *sheep* along with an army.'

There is a colourful account in Hoffstetter of the slaughter of some oxen bought just beyond Monterotondo, on the next day's march:

'Some farmers of the district had sold us twenty oxen for ready cash, eight of which were slaughtered at once. The beasts were tied together in a circle round a tree . . . then one of the South Americans, brought up on the prairies, took a dagger and very quickly stabbed one beast after another in the heart, with such precision that a second stroke was seldom needed, and the beast died almost at once. Naturally this extraordinary spectacle attracted a large crowd . . . the Commissariat shared out the meat among the troops, the most delicate pieces were reserved for the general . . . We lay on our saddles near the fire, cutting up the cooked bits with our daggers. But you could still read in some of the men's faces, longing for fat and salt.'

It was dark when we reached Mentana, its streets glistening with black rain, darker still when half an hour later, along a road whose tall poplar trees soughed and rustled and tipped, we wearily came to the gates of Monterotondo, and were directed towards a small *pensione* behind the cathedral.

'No good hoping to stay in the Franciscan monastery. Like *he* did
– or anyway his legion.'

'I certainly hope for something much less *frugal*.'

The *pensione*, its corridors lit by one bulb only – and briefly, too,
for it worked from a push-button near the door – had two
inestimable luxuries, beyond all words welcome to sodden
travellers: a kerosene stove, near whose brown enamelled pipes
could be dried, on backs of chairs, shoes, socks, shirts, trousers,
everything, *and*, not at all common in cheaper establishments,
showers whose water was hot and plentiful. As we dried and
warmed ourselves the noise of a school playground (no, this was
noisier than any school playground) came up to us from the
restaurant beneath.

It was a very large restaurant, every one of whose tables was
occupied by parties of children under twelve. Grown-ups were
hardly to be seen at all. I suppose we were conspicuous. But this was
a feast day for the children before Easter, and how busy and quick
and polite the waiters were, how excellent the food, no suggestion
that service was any laxer, dinner less delicious, than on any other
Saturday of the year!

'We will visit the fathers tomorrow, and take a last look at Rome.'

'The fathers, do you remember, nearly died of fright when
Garibaldi came. Don't *you* scare them.'

Pickets and sentinels were posted all around the monastery. But
the most alarming episode for the fathers must have been the
bungled execution. A soldier had been condemned to death for
insubordination, but before the sentence had been carried out, the
poor man broke his bonds, and ran as far as the gates of the
monastery, where he was arrested by the sentries. Only after a
terrible struggle was he finally shot.

'Not reassuring for them. Then there's the tale of Garibaldi
being able to order an execution without taking his cigar out of his
mouth.'

'But his soldiers were said to love him.'

'Very prudent of them.'

Early the next morning we climbed up the – now suburban –
road to the Franciscan monastery. I thought it wiser not to mention
Garibaldi when seeking admission. Even so, the voice through the
grille – the commonplace communication grille as spoken into in

any block of London flats – was not very welcoming. There was no aura of the mid-1800s. Requests for admission should be made to the Abbot, in writing. Thus rejected, we turned back to search for the lookout post nearby, where a staff officer had been posted with a good pair of binoculars, and had surveyed a tumble of small hills rich in vineyards and, beyond them, the flat expanse of the Campagna, on and on to the far-distant haze where there rose the majestic cupola of St Peter's. Hoffstetter again: 'Garibaldi held the cupola in a long, sad, fixed gaze. From a vineyard nearby could be heard a boy singing one of those passionate songs common in this countryside.'

No songs were sung for us. But after we had pushed back the branches of some fig trees, and scrambled to the top of the mound, and gazed out, tracking the curve of the earth's surface just as one can do at sea, there, indeed, nothing was visible in the distance, no skyscrapers, no cities, no motorways, nothing at all save that very faint but unmistakable dome, sliced off by the knife of the horizon; and we could feel the sorrow of the moment, and the vow to return.

'But *did* he ever come back?'

'Yes, of course, in sixteen years' time – to Mentana, anyway. And that was a disaster, a massacre almost. You remember the French chassepots . . .'

These were the new breech-loading rifles named after their inventor Major Chassepot. Needles fired the cartridges. Garibaldi's rustily-armed irregulars were routed in 1866, so that Papal Rome was in the end 'liberated' only because its French defenders were withdrawn to fight in the Franco-Prussian war: Bismarck (in a sense) succeeded where Garibaldi failed.

Slants of rain hid the distant dome, while we were still desultorily warming and drying ourselves in the uneasy morning sunlight.

'We – or anyway I – must go to speak to Signor Ferrante.'

This was the local historian whose name had kindly been given to us at our *pensione*. A most courteous voice had explained to me on the telephone that his father was just then in his studio, but I had secured an appointment for nine-thirty.

The address, however, was difficult to find. Windows were thrown open above me as I groped around. A lady shouted, 'Signor Ferrante? You are looking for a haircut?'

'I am looking for the historian. The professor.'

She shut the window. Ferrante was probably a common name in

the town. Or there may have been some political or family feuds which, as in Tivoli, led to avowals of non-existence of certain people. I went back to the corner café.

'Signor Ferrante? Number twenty-six. He should be open for his first clients soon.'

This seemed to suggest that he gave tutorials on a fairly regular basis. Yet his name was not to be seen on any of the cards in the entrance of the apartment block. With irresponsible abandon I rang all the bells, one after the other.

Signor Ferrante, fortunately, was the only inhabitant to run down to greet me. Others, who opened their windows, were mollified by him. Within five minutes or less he had rolled up the Saracen shutters of his barber's shop and had placed on my knee three fat volumes of scrapbooks. I asked him, to start with, why Monterotondo was described in one of the guidebooks as 'the Paris of the Sabine Hills'. There were no night clubs, no Eiffel Tower, no Hilton Hotel even? No river, no left bank, no right bank? He agreed that it seemed an exaggeration. He took refuge behind a quotation from a book in the Alexandrian Library of Rome – then, coming closer to Garibaldi, he insisted, 'This has always been a town very loyal to the Church. There is a legend that St Peter himself set foot in Monterotondo before he reached Rome.'

'Supported the Church even in the days of the Roman Republic?'

'Especially then. Garibaldi was only a hero later.'

How easy it is to forget that Garibaldi in 1849 was little more than a leader of a guerrilla band, a hero who had formed an Italian legion to fight obscure battles, in exile, on the prairies of Uruguay: who the year before had offered his services to Piedmont, and captured a couple of paddle-steamers on Lake Maggiore!

He had led his alarming band of irregulars into Monterotondo on July 4th, his forty-second birthday. Why on earth did he believe, or even hope, that he might be able to arouse the local population and *'fare una bella guerra'*? There was no great agrarian unrest, no passionate hatreds to stir up in these small towns. On the contrary, there were quite a few clerical supporters, and many more Moderates or Constitutionalists who had been thoroughly antagonized by the flurry of laws and edicts and taxes coming from the Republican triumvirs – to say nothing of the political assassinations. Again, why should anyone risk fighting for a lost cause and perhaps be excommunicated into the bargain? The prudent would have learnt a lesson from the Austrian victory at Novara earlier that year; and from the successful counter-revolution in Tuscany and the restoration of the Grand Duke. No – one can only conclude that Garibaldi was so deeply in love with the idea of Republican Italy One and Indivisible, had such fervent faith that Italy *must* one day be freed from the rule of the Pope and of the other Sovereigns, that he allowed his grasp of the practical to be weakened by the rhetoric of Mazzini and others. 'What use to lose time in vain formality?' he had shouted in the first meeting of the National Assembly in February. 'The delay of even a minute is a crime. Long Live the REPUBLIC!'

Signor Ferrante was not of course intending to disparage Garibaldi, even if this was the general line of our conversation. He was alive to the other side of the General – his utter honesty, his amazing courage, his readiness to renounce worldly rewards. 'You realize he called one of his donkeys, on that island of his, by the name of Pio Nono?' he said, going over to the wash-basin to sort out his clippers and razors for his first *real* client.

❦ IV ❦
Poggio Mirteto
(6–7 July)

WE WALKED DOWN FROM MONTEROTONDO towards the Tiber and to the town's railway halt, in the familiar rain. Yet this may give a misleading impression. The deluge was such that it felt as though we were swept down the steep hill in an engulfing flood. Buffets of wind made the branches of poplars wave and toss furiously, tore open the flap of a rucksack. Three kilometres brought us to the deserted platform, enlivened by the passage of continental expresses whistling past.

'Just up there is the bridge which puts you on to the road to Viterbo.'

'The Ponte del Grillo. Cricket bridge. Insect, not game.'

Here, I take it, was the ford which the Polish Major Muller must have crossed, at the head of his fifty horse, in order to lead the enemy into thinking that Garibaldi was heading towards the Tyrrhenian coast. To deceive, the secret was always to deceive. One feint east at Tivoli, one feint west here. But, after leaving Monterotondo at three o'clock in the morning of July 5th, the General led the main body *northwards* up the valley of the Tiber, and after a brief march, made the 'midday' stop on the far side of a great stone bridge.

The scene as Hoffstetter describes it: 'The Tiber runs here in a narrow valley, green and shady; its fresh waters invited us all to bathe. The troops stayed this side of the river, the staff crossed it, to rest under a rock, where the signora of Garibaldi had already dismounted . . . The horses were very hungry and fed on leaves and shrubs.'

We had taken the local train one stop, to give us time to search for this shady place: ourselves perhaps to picnic there.

'Your Austrian military map is useless. No bridges over the Tiber anywhere near here.'

37

'Trevelyan thinks it must be the Passo Correse, or more likely the Ponte Sfondato over the Farfa.'

'We will ask the locals.'

We walked up a long, narrow valley, in the folds of which some good-looking young chestnut horses stood disconsolate in the shelter of brambly hedges. As we passed one or two of them kicked up their heels and made a brief but spirited canter. Their hooves squelched. There was nothing else in sight.

'Where did Trevelyan think this bridge was?'

'Something about it being in a wild, narrow and rocky wooded valley, and it could easily be called a great stone bridge, because it's the living rock through which the Farfa burrows its way.'

'*Living rock?*'

'That's what he says.'

Since I had talked to Signor Ferrante that morning, it seemed appropriate to think of historians as we emerged from our own wooded valley – not I fear the same one – and began to walk along the level. I like to keep a certain respectful distance from Trevelyan: his immensely powerful and colourful *Defence of the Roman Republic* is a great *tour de force*, but I was anxious to see the Retreat not through his eyes, but through my own – and Hoffstetter's.

Writing in the high noon of Liberal enthusiasm for the Italian Risorgimento, Trevelyan could allow Garibaldi to do no wrong. He saw the great Liberator of Italy as a knight in shining armour, *sans peur* and (almost) *sans reproche*. Indeed, he tells in his auto-biography how his method of writing history sprang from his youthful passion:

'Love of poetry has affected the character and in places the style of my historical writings, and in part dictated my choice of subjects. Garibaldi attracted me because his life seemed to me the most poetical of all true stories, and I tried to preserve a little of this quality in telling the tale in prose.'

So we continued to cast about in search of the great stone bridge. I should still like to see where Anita sat, sewing a tent. But outside one of those vast modern furniture stores, or permanent exhibitions as they are called, which arise mysteriously far outside any town, and even on secondary roads in remote quarters of Italy, we found two fairly old men who were willing to listen, with great patience, to

my questions. The maps were laid out on an iron garden-table.
They answered,

'Old bridge? All the bridges around here are old.'

'Old *stone* bridge. In the time of Garibaldi?'

'All the bridges round here were destroyed by the Germans in
the war.'

In the distance, at the bottom of another wooded valley
beneath us, I could dimly see a long, soulless bridge with cement
pillars. If we descended here, we would certainly reach the Farfa.
On the other hand, Poggio Mirteto still lay two hours ahead of us,
and above us. Alas for temptation! We looked at the skies, and
looked east and west, and were suddenly rewarded, beyond our
deserts, by a sight that Garibaldi, in the sweltering heat of
July, could not possibly have seen: snow lying on the saw-tooth
peaks of Soracte, on the far side of the Tiber. This is a
mountain, 2500 feet of jagged limestone which, arising solitary
from the plain, looks higher and stranger than its height suggests:
on a clear day easily to be seen from Rome, twenty-five miles to the
south.

'You remember, of course, those lines of Horace?'

'Vides ut alta stet nive candidum.'

'You must have looked it up before.'

Yes . . . well. The snowy teeth looked carved, two-dimensional.
Constantly, as we wound uphill on roads that led between long
slopes, sweet and covered with vineyards (as Hoffstetter says),
Soracte came back, back again into our vision, and as the afternoon
turned into gentle evening, the snow became rose.

We took several short-cuts. One hollow, shell-shaped head of a
valley, out of which bubbled the spring of a Tiber tributary, was
called on the map 'arcone': a not uncommon name for such hollows,
easily to be imagined as enormous, upturned bows.

'This is a fairly gentle walk.'

'Not too hard for *him*, either. Poggio Mirteto is only about
twenty-five kilometres from Monterotondo.'

For Garibaldi was no longer racing, as he had done at first. His
scouts would have told him he was not being pursued along the
roads which led north from Rome. A Spanish army was indeed
marching northwards too – but that was towards Rieti, along a
parallel valley fifteen miles to the east. One French army, deceived

by his first feints, was drawing a blank, rummaging east of Rome in the forests and mountains of the Abruzzi: another one was travelling west to the Tyrrhenian Sea to fall upon him should he attempt to embark from that shore. Meanwhile he was marching between his enemies up the Tiber, calmly and as yet unharassed.

'Another reason for his going slowly was that he was still making rough saddles for all the mules. He was looking forward to getting rid of the carts.'

'If only he'd been as politically cunning as he was militarily!'

'What soldier ever has been?'

It was indeed a particularly easy march for them that evening. The baggage train left the cool riverbank at midnight, the main body two hours later. Fodder had arrived and the horses were fed – Hoffstetter feeding his two with oats from his beret. The moon was full. Instead of the evening review the soldiers had been given heart by a brief and juicy harangue from their General. They loved him as much as they feared him. He knew only two punishments – reprimand and death.

'I don't think I should like to have been reprimanded by him one little bit.'

'Does Hoffstetter really say *juicy* harangue?'

'That's what *succoso* means.'

We were sitting on a low stone wall, on the outskirts of Montopoli in Sabina – a polite township, with a long avenue of pollarded trees, and evidence of one or two week-end villas. Poggio Mirteto was only a half-hour away now, on the next hilltop. The General did better than us, though; for he arrived in the early morning, and was brought an excellent breakfast by the Chief Magistrate's wife, complete with a delicious fruit salad, with early, big, black figs.

She presided over the breakfast, too, and did the honours of the table in the most graceful and charming way.

Garibaldi meanwhile sent out a platoon of cavalry north-east to the monastery of San Valentino, and both horse and foot were sent to stand guard on the road to Rome. Not least important, Anita was despatched to rest with a family in a house in the main square of Poggio Mirteto.

It was here, in the dusk, that we looked at the plaque telling of her stay, before we entered and groped our way up the dark staircase of what is, now, a small hotel. How politely we were told that, alas, no room was to be had! This was a most disappointing, tired moment.

Poggio Mirteto (6-7 July)

If Anita had stayed here, so should we. Rejected, we stood outside, translating aloud the memorial description:

> In this house of the family Lattanze
> Anita Garibaldi,
> On the 6th and 7th July 1849
> lovingly welcomed,
> had rest and refreshment.
> Together with the throb of maternity
> there beat in her heroic heart
> the dream of Rome
> and perhaps like a sunset light there came to her
> the Annunciation of Death.

'I think I shall go back and throw myself on the woman's mercy, and explain the pilgrimage we're on. She can't refuse us.'

'How embarrassing! *I* shall try to find the café which Hoffstetter says was kept by a Swiss – so that he was able to have a conversation in German for about an hour.'

I was extremely grateful when the proprietress relented: sneakily pleased, too, at being able to win more sympathy than incredulity with my tale. Even though she had no room to give us, her son would drive us two miles to the outskirts, where there were several beds and, she thought, even hot water. Then we could come back to supper. Meanwhile, we must have a drink.

One shutter of the dark dining room was opened. On the walls hung ancient oleographs of the Italian lakes. In a corner a vast bird cage hung from the ceiling on a tasselled cord. An old pack of cards lay on a linoleum tablecloth. From one of the occupied rooms came the sound of gentle, heaving, regular snores.

She disappeared to fetch us white wine. She seemed quite as kind as the Chief Magistrate's wife.

'Where are the other guests? It's not exactly all *happening* at this hotel.'

'There are some boards creaking. I think somebody else must be awake.'

An immensely ancient, tall man, with rheumy eyes, walked in and sat at the table by the cards, hanging his stick on the back of his chair. He gave us a smile of great sweetness, and appeared to fall asleep immediately.

'A Garibaldino, do you think?'

'Oh no. Much, much too *old* to have fought in 1849.'

We finished our small decanter of white wine. Three more old men, one of whom might have been just under eighty, joined the sleeping man at the card table. They played without speaking; their game had a spectral quality: a slow-motion rite seen refracted, as though under water, in the dimly-lit room.

'Those are gas fittings, surely?'

'Do you think the card players will be here when we come back?'

'They are Rip Van Winkles.'

The landlady's son drove us, as promised, to our rooms. He believed that the block of apartments was very near Garibaldi's encampment – and certainly it was in the right direction – but I suspect that he wished to please us. Five double bedrooms led off a long corridor. Of other occupants there was no sign, save for a rusty razor, on a cobwebbed mantelshelf.

'I refuse to travel any longer with a bearded, delinquent youth.'

'I shall take a very long, hot bath. I might even shave.'

When we walked back in the moonlight, across the head of a small valley, past a tall, gaunt building which looked like an old mill, the smell of charcoal cooking filled the air. Nothing very much could have changed in some of these streets, nothing very much either in the dark passages of our hotel where the kind family gave Anita food and rest, and where she herself had washed and mended her clothes. Before the great chimney-piece of the restaurant the proprietress's mother – over a hundred we were told with pride – sat motionless near a black cauldron. All the tables were occupied by the peers of the first very old man, save for the one next to ours, where a turbaned lady actually moved: that is to say, she arranged and rearranged her knife and fork. No one spoke.

Dinner passed as in a dream. Dream? There was one passage of nightmare. A large bird, an overfed turtledove I believe, fluttered from its cage and swooped round and round the room. This flight at first attracted no notice. Perhaps it was a regular attraction. Then our turbaned neighbour made a few appropriate noises – clucking, I suppose, for those who cannot whistle, being the best method of addressing birds. She rose, and executed a slow dance in the middle of the room, underneath the hanging gaslight.

'Is that a pavane?'

'Surely something less sprightly?'

Poggio Mirteto (6-7 July)

'But pavane *is* a slow, stately dance. Like peacocks.'

As she moved, the bird alighted on the top of her turban. She clapped her hands. From one table to another she walked, stooping to point at the living ornament on her hat. The bird looked down upon us as we ate our tagliatelle. It was difficult to think of any suitable compliment. Should one clap? Raise one's fork and shout '*Bravissimo*'?

At last she returned to sit at her own table. But the bird continued to perch on her. I could see its claws. Her head nodded as she ate.

'Has it occurred to you that this is not a hotel at all?'

'??'

'It is a *pensione* for the elderly – a Hotel Methuselah.'

'Ah, that would certainly explain a great deal. The bird is probably a very old bird, too.'

And might this also account for a confusion over the bill, a reluctance indeed to present it at all? The landlady's table had been enlivened by the arrival of a dazzling granddaughter, or great-granddaughter, who bestowed kisses everywhere; but even she did not seem to know the correct charge. In the end, there was unanimous refusal to take more than ten pounds for dinner and bed for the two of us. There was a long wait while a large black money-box was opened, and change found in coins.

'*Money.* I can't make out our hero's attitude towards it.'

'Fairly close, I think. As with information.'

We know that when Garibaldi left Rome, he took with him a strongbox containing 'enough paper money for 4000 men for a month'. This was voted to him as one of the last acts of the triumvirate which had taken over to negotiate the surrender. (More important, the strongbox contained the decree giving him full powers as the legal representative of a republic not yet dead.) This paper money of the Republic was subsequently honoured only at sixty-five per cent of its face value, but Garibaldi cannot be blamed for that.

As Hoffstetter says, 'If one counts this behaviour as robbery then all the generals great and small since the revolution of 1789 – including Napoleon himself – were robbers too. Every so often we issued coupons which were gladly accepted; and the locals told us that news had come from Rome that the coupons of Garibaldi would all be honoured: a very reasonable act by the new government. When the General heard that in future the republican

43

paper-money had to be re-stamped in Rome to have currency, he found means indirectly to get it there.'

Strange, indeed! Many of the *buoni* or coupons can still be found, in archives, and even in private possession.

'Ah, here it is at last – our change.'

'I think we can reasonably leave all the tinkling coins.'

Not that this would have been Garibaldi's attitude at all. For it was at Poggio Mirteto that he first began to change paper money into coins; and there is some evidence to suggest that, about now, he may have begun to contemplate his optimistic excursion into Tuscany – knowing that Roman paper money would be of no use in the Grand Duchy.

Meanwhile, in two days' time, he was to meet the Englishman Forbes (and his son) in Terni, at the head of his four hundred men who had marched from Urbino.

V

Terni

(8-9 July)

THE ENGLISHMAN FORBES! What strange chain of events led this forty-one-year-old Old Etonian and ex-Coldstream officer to fight, in his white top-hat, for the revolutionary cause of the Roman Republic? It is true that he belonged to a family which, as Admiral Forbes wrote to his great-nephew the 6th Earl of Granard, 'has from all times been addicted to the use of arms'. True, too, that the Forbes soldiers and sailors have been of independent spirit – their Irish origins perhaps – and have found themselves in some remarkable situations: Admiral Forbes himself refused to be party to the execution of poor Byng, and another forebear was offered the post of supreme commander of the Russian Navy by the Czarina in 1704.

But to become a silk merchant in Siena, to call himself an 'earnest red republican', to join forces with Garibaldi? Later to become a fencing-master in New York, and in charge of drill instruction for John Brown, and a beggar? At last – having fought once more for Garibaldi in Sicily – to die poor, but mourned, in Pisa?

We were walking along a small track westwards out of Poggio Mirteto, back down into the valley of the Tiber. Cypresses lined the switchback road as far as the cemetery, recalling, together with the thought of Forbes's end, those lines of Garibaldi's favourite poet, champion of Italy in Napoleon's time, Ugo Foscolo.

> All' ombra di cipressi e dentro l'urne
> confortate di pianto è forse il sonno
> della morte men duro?

> The sleep of death – is it less grim within
> Those tombs where tears bring comfort, and beneath
> The shade of cypresses?

The Englishman Forbes! Trevelyan, in his later editions of the *Defence of the Roman Republic*, had access to papers from a descendant of Forbes which, alas, I can nowhere trace. I know only that he was a member of the Granard family because the papers relating to the purchase of his commission, in the Public Record Office, show that Admiral Forbes's two daughters, Lady Clarendon and Lady Maryborough, wrote on his behalf as a 'relative'. HRH the Duke of Cambridge assisted, and the matter was settled in the summer of 1826, with a lodgement of £1100 at Greenwood, Cox and Company.

Five years later, on March 3rd 1831, Lt Forbes appears for the last time on duty in Horse Guards Parade, in Capt. Bentinck's company: in July he retired on half-pay as Captain. Let Trevelyan by all means refer to him as Colonel (which he was, indeed, in the Republican army), I prefer to call him by his own style of 'Citizen Colonel'.

'And how far are we now before we reach Cantalupo where one of the Citizen Colonel's aides was sent to meet our man?'

'At least an hour.'

We had by now crossed a ford, and were walking up a long road northwards, through deserted and most beautiful countryside, copses of beech and of birch set on small hillocks, shafts of sun lighting up the white towers and houses of distant Roccantica and of other Sabine hill-towns, so that they beckoned like one Celestial City after the other.

For the stretch after Cantalupo the General, more prudent than ourselves, had taken plenty of meat and bread for his men; having foreseen, or been warned, that provisions would be hard to find on the way, no oxen to buy and slaughter.

This march of theirs lasted from two in the morning until mid-day, was very wearying and intensely hot, though Hoffstetter still found time to notice that the road was 'magnificent, the surrounding country enormously rich in vineyards'. Always with an eye to the wine! They became very thirsty. The beds of the streams and torrents were all dry. At Vacone there was one fountain with enough water only for the occasional passer-by. And then, at last, they came to Configni! Here, underneath the village, there still may be seen a great trough – though if it is the same one, its splendour has faded a little from the days when Hoffstetter could describe it as follows:

'. . . before pitching our camp, we had to allow the soldiers to quench their thirst; they all crowded round the natural drink. Most ravenous of all were the horses, some of whom clambered up with their front hoofs into the trough. My morel was the eagerest of them all, burying his head up to his eyes in the water . . .

'. . . These fountains are divided into two parts: one small, arched portion collects water for the men: the water in this then runs into a long, deep trough, hollowed out of rock, where one can water twenty beasts at a time.'

Immensely thirsty ourselves, we had arrived here after a late lunch in Torre, a tiny walled town nearby, whose promenade is bounded on one side by a sheer fall into vineyards, and on the other by a row of low houses built into the rock: one of these was an anonymous trattoria, excellent, crowded, dark – little more than a. cave burrowing in the hillside.

'Don't think I'm complaining, but this isn't up to the Forbes standard of luxury.'

'I suppose you think we should stay in the Hotel Europa in Terni, like he did?'

'Why not? You are extraordinarily mean, my dear father. Forbes *et fils* did much better than us.'

His son was about twenty years old. Though he had by now spent some years of his life in Italy, he could still speak no Italian at all: later in the march, he was to cry tears of rage and frustration when nobody could be made to understand his fear that he had lost his much-loved white mule, his desperate desire to retrieve it.

One of the aristocratic tastes which the red revolutionist had retained, was for staying in the best hotels. This was in contrast to his General, who almost always shared the discomfort – and the pleasures – of the camp with his men; and sometimes would tell tales round the camp fire late into the night, about his South American adventures. Here is one of them, as told by Hoffstetter.

'". . . in a war in the forests and on the immense prairies, there are no regular bodies of men . . . *condottieri* like me might find themselves one day at the head of 3000 men, the next day only of 300. Sometimes I had a platoon of cavalry as fast as the wind . . . Once I found myself after a bitter cavalry fight, left with only 800 men, of whom half were foot soldiers . . . And then we were attacked by a much stronger enemy force and put to flight after a furious battle. I managed to reach the safety of the forest with only 400

47

men. My wife was fighting on the left wing . . . her hat was shot through by a bullet, her horse was killed beneath her and she was taken prisoner. But in the night, after her captors had gone to sleep and even her guards began to snore, this brave woman freed herself, caught a horse and fled. She was followed almost at once by several horsemen, but charged into a broad river and, holding on to her horse's tail, swam to the other side despite a hail of bullets from behind her. She knew only very roughly the direction I had taken; and, all alone, rode through virgin forests for four days and nights, with no food of any sort. She found me only after eight days. We were near to starving too; on the fourth day we came out of the forest on to a plateau, where the rice was being cooked for the slaves. The famished men flung themselves on to cauldrons, filled their hands and ate the rice, boiling, just as it was. Yes, gentlemen, my wife is a very valiant lady," finished the General, holding out his hand to her and giving her a look full of affection. Joy and pride shone from her face.'

For the last few miles into Terni, city of steel and armament manufacture, we hitch-hiked, asking to be dropped at the monastery of St Valentine where Garibaldi, his staff and the infantry took their lodging – without, I imagine, very much ceremony.

How delighted Hoffstetter was, after so many days of village comforts, to come at last to a proper city!

'We walked happily among the spacious streets and squares of the town, in front of the grand hotels and cafés, on to the pleasant gardens outside the city walls. No fear of disorders, because drunkenness is almost unknown among Italian soldiers: on the other hand they did enjoy sipping once again their lemonades and their coffee, or taking a sorbet . . . and eyeing the pretty girls.'

Terni is dedicated to St Valentine, *il Santo d'innamorati*, and does seem to have more than its share of pretty girls. They came in clusters, arm-in-arm, round the corners of the streets, glanced and laughed. All this Hoffstetter enjoyed as much as we did. The only whisper – faint, faint whisper – of disloyalty towards the General, occurs now, when he writes, 'I was not able to leave the saddle till three hours after halting, and this time I declined the modest table of the general, to be able to eat better in the city.'

'I do think we might follow his example – unless you're still feeling mean.'

'All right. Choose between an expensive hotel, a good restaurant: greed and comfort.'

'Greed.'

In any case Forbes's luxury Hotel Europa is no more. But a simple, clean *pensione* with a splendid façade, the Albergo Roma, overlooks the square where the baggage train was drawn up, and where they worked hard at restoring everything to order.

Although the Republic had now fallen for several days, its writ still ran here in Terni, thanks to Citizen Colonel Forbes. The tree of Liberty, symbol of revolutionary freedom, was still in the main square. The pretty girls wore tricolour ribbons in their hair, tricolour flags hung from the windows of the palazzi.

Forbes, however, was not popular. This lover of liberty, dry, always clean-shaven, severe, '*vero tipo inglese*', was an extra-ordinarily strict disciplinarian. His men had lately drawn their sabres when the population had dared to show their discontent, their resentment at his everlasting requisitions of 'harness, shoes, provisions and money, always money, even although a very considerable forced loan had already been exacted from the church'.

But what angered the citizens of Terni more than his constant demands, more than threats of execution if they were not met, more than the high-handedness of a man who ended his letters of extortion with expressions of love and fraternity, was his proposal to blow up the main bridge of the city, over the Nera: a most beautiful bridge, and extremely expensive to rebuild.

Forbes clearly set store by appearance as well as on discipline: he had managed to provide uniforms for his battalion, made up of Swiss, of revenue officers and of the remains of the Papal army that had fought the Austrians in Lombardy (a scratch side indeed), consisting of light grey blouses and trousers, with red facings; and a high hat (or kepi, like the Foreign Legion used to wear) of waxed canvas.

Elegant though he may have been, and devoted to the cause of Italian liberty as he saw it, he was clearly a man of considerable violence. Take this passage from his book *The Volunteer's Manual (Being the art of winning and maintaining Liberty and Independence)* published in New York six years later, in 1855.

'The early practice of boxing habituates the youth to despise whatever is unfair and ingenuous (as did the tournaments of the

49

middle ages), instils into them endurance and perseverance, and in after life makes the soldier feel at home in those hand-to-hand fights which in war occasionally occur; and in which, from the close contact with the enemy, the only hope of safety lies in victory; deciding sometimes not only the fate of a single battle, but even of a campaign, upon which may depend the fate of a nation for many generations.'

I especially like the phrase 'feel at home'. Another notion of the flavour of the book may be had from the index; following on the heels of BATTER there runs, BAYONET-BIVOUAC-BLOW DOWN WALL OR GATE-BLOW UP-BOLDNESS (WHEN PRUDENT)-BOTTLES.

The book may be unjustly neglected by the guerrilla of today. Much of it reads to me like very good sense. Possibly it is too elementary. But can one catch echoes of the late Chairman Mao's doctrines from pasaages like this?

'. . . a multiplicity of little bands, some three to ten miles distant from each other, yet in connection and communication, CANNOT be surrounded especially in a chain of well-wooded mountains such as the Apennines.' And ties 'The Central Committee . . . will provide necessarily for the Guerrilla, collecting the means through the local committees, with the least possible injury to the populations. It must keep alive the democratic spirit among the population because the war of insurrection must lean for support upon the popular element – or it will fail.'

It seemed perfectly appropriate to discuss the red revolutionist's ideas over the best dinner which Terni could provide: one which Forbes would himself have approved. It can't be denied that his style is vigorous: a loss to the Coldstream.

'I particularly like that bit when he says that he wishes that there were a few more revolutionists in Europe who instead of *composing poetry*, would write plain commonsense.'

'I looked up bottles – by the way, don't you think we might run to another one now? – and he said you could do a lot of damage with *broken* bottles. He would have made a good Chelsea supporter.'

I'm afraid the Terni archives – generous with his time though the archivist was – showed up little more about the Citizen Colonel. Yet it does at least seem that for all his high-handedness, Forbes was scrupulous in paying his small debts for the continual horses he commandeered (even if the money was derived from extortions). The most interesting entry for July '49 is the engagement by Garibaldi himself, on the same day as he entered Terni, of 49 one-horse carts to travel to Todi: by far the largest single piece of commandeering of the year. It suggests an immediate decision on arrival in the city to abandon any lingering idea of striking east or north-east, and taking ship to Venice from a port south of Ancona. He had intelligence from his cavalry scouts that the Austrians were blocking the main road which leads north to Spoleto and Foligno. Neither they nor he seemed eager for a battle at this point. Hoffstetter believes Garibaldi hoped to draw the Austrians on after him into Tuscany and thus to free a passage over the main Apennines to Rimini.

And the carts? They were presumably the same ones to which Hoffstetter refers: loaded with bread and provisions, they were to trundle out on the road to Todi the day after Garibaldi left Terni. Their hope to rely on mules had suffered a setback: the animals were worn out by the heat and the forced marches, and the harness had given them frightful sores. Indeed they smelt so badly, and were so difficult to manage, that two soldiers attended each beast, one leading, the other looking after the load: for this disagreeable task they were paid double rates.

We ourselves walked from the outskirts of Terni gently uphill to the gates of St Gemini arriving dry and covered with white dust blown from a quarry. Resting, near the city, in the shade of an olive tree we followed the trail of a most laborious march head-to-tail along the road of no fewer than sixty-six caterpillars who turned, slowly, down along a road which led to a cemetery. We counted them.

'Forbes would have approved of their discipline.'

'Or would he have smashed them up?'

In his Volunteer's Guide he issued precise instructions for procedure on all occasions. For example – appropriate now to record – for funerals:

'In the centre of the column will be carried the corpse, the pall being carried by comrades of the same rank, the relations and particular friends following immediately after the corpse (in regularity and not confusedly) . . .'

A volunteer's life, under the Citizen Colonel, was strict to the very end.

VI

San Gemini and Cesi
(9-10 July)

T HE GENERAL LEFT TERNI LATE IN THE AFTERNOON of July
9th, having attended to various affairs in the city. By then the
main body, including Forbes and his men who formed the second
legion, were well on the road, so he galloped after them: or rather, as
usual when in haste, he galloped his horse for five minutes, and
walked it for one. He was always considerate to animals, one of
the characteristics which, later in life, was to endear him to the
British.

He found his troops camped in a large, flat field near a fountain,
at a fork from which one road leads steeply uphill to Cesi, the other
to the neighbouring hill of San Gemini.

At eleven in the evening they were pleasantly surprised by a
deputation who came down from Cesi, to present them with a large
butt of wine which Hoffstetter claims was the best he had ever
tasted.

'That must be the goal of our walk to Cesi. I expect they still
make it.'

'I don't want to sound stingy, but I'm not sure we could manage
a butt.'

 Like the advance cavalry, we had left Terni early, and had
passed the broad, flat field at noon. But we were considerably more
comfortably billeted than they were – for we chose to stay in the
elegant Albergo Duomo of San Gemini, which has access to the
delectable cathedral gardens: tall pines, mazes of well-kept shrubs,
glades with white wooden seats, circles of rose-beds, smell of box-
leaves.

We had plenty of time to walk down the deep valley, across the
streams which lead to the fountain of the encampment, and up
through wooded paths to the small town of Cesi. We entered the
Commune.

'They will know all about Garibaldi's visit here.'

'I am ready for the wine.'

We were received in the Commune most courteously, as always. My speech about the footsteps of the General was listened to patiently. The Mayor's secretary spoke at last, with care.

'I believe there is an inscription at Acquasparta, eight kilometres on.'

'But memories here? The excellent wine? Ugo Bassi's stay?'

'No wine is made at Cesi now – none at least that you will find for sale.'

We were coming to a dead end. Desperately I asked for news of an inscription, a statue, a square, a street even.

'There are no inscriptions here. None at all. No street, no square after Garibaldi.' As the Mayor spoke, the secretary nodded.

'But there are at San Gemini.' That was a foolish thing for me to have blurted out. I had forgotten possible local rivalries. The Mayor shrugged his shoulders.

Any goodwill that might have attached to an English 'historian' on however eccentric an errand, was dwindling. What happened or not, or was remembered or not, in San Gemini was no affair of his. He was very sorry. He looked at his watch. I did not dare even to pursue the subject of local wine-making traditions.

Leaving his office, it was by accident that I glanced upwards, to a large plaque occupying almost half one wall of the entrance hall, and translated.

> In the glorious sunset
> of the Roman Republic
> Giuseppe Garibaldi stayed here
> on the eleventh of July 1849.
> May this humble memorial record,
> for the reverence of the people,
> the footsteps of the hero.

'Like that story of the lost letter of Edgar Allan Poe's.'

'Possibly. So familiar an object he's stopped noticing it altogether.'

'Unless he just wanted to get rid of us.'

'Or couldn't understand your Italian.'

Since to discover the true explanation would have been too

discourteous, we returned to the search of the legendary Cesi wine. Persistence alas was not rewarded. But the *water*, we were assured, was certainly the best in Italy. We ought to climb to the Fountain of Living Water that sprang from the hillside 200 metres above the town. And only a little further on, near the great Roman ruins of Carsulae, there was the source of the finest Acqua Minerale in the world.

But the sun was setting, and all we could do today was to walk downhill and overlook once more that field of encampment and that other fountain.

'Do you remember where Hoffstetter tells of the astonishment of Forbes's men when they heard that Garibaldi used to sleep in the open, on his saddle-covering? But that today he was sleeping in that house up there, where the light was burning?'

Garibaldi had laughed loudly when he was told of this and prophesied that Forbes's men may not have been used to living like that, but they soon would be. And so, indeed, they were except for all those men who had stayed behind in Terni and those others who, day after day, slunk away. Some of the dragoons and other horsemen – not only Forbes's – were tempted to desert by the value of their horses: these desertions sowed the seed of a discontent which was soon to become general.

By contrast our own contentment was growing. There is a great deal to be said for San Gemini: within its walls there is no disharmony, far indeed from its description in *Murray's Guide* of 1857 as 'a miserable place of 1500 souls'.

The Mayor, upon whom we called next morning, most obligingly unlocked the door of a lumber room and took down from its long-undisturbed resting-place above a cupboard, a dirty portfolio containing some dozens of manifesti, or wall posters, belonging to the period of the Roman Republic. One of these was printed in San Gemini in May '49 and read,

'The Municipal council . . . through the work of you, the triumvirs . . . send to France the message that it is wrong to trample upon the weak, and that the soldier of the Roman Republic carries in his breast the wound inflicted by the Austrian Gaoler.'

Forlorn – this appeal from a tiny municipality to the forbearance of the French, this attempt of David's to remind Goliath that the Roman Republic's natural enemy was Austria, enemy of Liberty!

And then there is an inscription, over the entrance gate to the city, placed there a year after Garibaldi's death, to commemorate his brief passage. The Mayor told us that until recent times an ancient devotee of Garibaldi would take his grandson every morning dutifully to bow to the plaque, much as a worshipper might bow towards Mecca.

Later that morning we walked on northwards, through Umbrian countryside whose greens, pale and dark, were illuminated by spring sunshine, towards a ridge where mineral waters spring, and flow with such abundance that taps are left open so that any passerby may fill a few bottles free and even bathe his face in the cool, pure waters. From here, it is only a few minutes' walk to the site of the ancient Roman settlement of Carsulae, where Hoffstetter experienced some moments of magic, ecstasy almost.

'. . . this reconnaissance satisfied the military eye because of the favourable lie of the land. These irregular heights, rocky and covered with shrubs, negotiable by horses only with difficulty, were almost made for us . . . and enemy cavalry and artillery would be forced to travel along roads.

'But not only that. The eye, greedy for beauty, was rewarded with the most magnificent views. Gilded by the rays of the early sun, there lay at our feet, rising out of the vivid green of vineyards, the cities of Cesi, Narni, San Gemini, Terni: while from the far-off haze of mountains emerged new castles, along the wide sweep of the horizon. On the ground where we stood, there was once a Sabine city. Still now, scattered here and there on the remote and solitary site, lie the ruins of enormous blocks of stone, broken fragments of fountains and of columns. One great gate stands all alone in the midst of the ruins.

'Underneath this arch the General passed in silence. From a man dressed in a toga whom we saw before us, was anything missing except the helmet, to turn him into a Roman consul? Garibaldi was silent and grave. No one dared here to address a word to him. Everyone passed into a dream. And truly our life and actions were as extraordinary and as poetic as could possibly be. Fatigue, hunger, thirst, privations of every kind, mortal dangers and then the most sublime exaltations.'

The ghosts of Roman consuls may well stalk these ruins; for although scarcely mentioned in the histories of Rome, Carsulae was a very considerable settlement indeed, lying just one day and one night's march north from Rome. Troops making for the Adriatic provinces, travelling say to Fano (which was the Fanum Fortunae or Temple of Fortune of the Empire), must have used Carsulae as one of their first staging-posts. To have made a votive offering at the end of the first day's arduous march, in the temples of Courage and of Honour (underneath one of whose arches Garibaldi rode eighteen centuries later), would have given them encouragement and strength for the next stage: and the pure water, refreshment.

Our own and Garibaldi's next stage became rather confused; for now the General decided to fan his troops in more directions than ever. To have platoons of cavalry appear here, there and everywhere was an essential part of his tactics of deception. Garibaldini (some of them impostors) were seen in Acquasparta, Acquaforte, Settivalle and other towns. And we ourselves in the recurring rain took the single-track branch line to Acquasparta from which, on this and the following day, we walked in all directions of the compass too, using the small town as a base: acting like scouts.

That evening we found ourselves on the balcony of a small *pensione* underneath the arches of whose first floor hung a long line of washing. We had just passed, as we walked up from the station, a scene as rich in ghosts as Hoffstetter could have wished.

Three old men sat at a crossroads in the lumpy moquette armchairs of a second- or third-hand furniture shop: sat silent and still, one of them wearing a kepi like those of Forbes's officers, all of them bearded like true Garibaldini.

'Waiting for Godot?'

'You see the one with drooping moustache? Rather like an old picture of the Kaiser?'

Perhaps this was the ghost of the Austrian officer who was captured near here in disguise, and whom Garibaldi, despite many appeals from his men, declined to shoot. For he was far from being ungenerous or merciless towards his enemies, reserving his strict punishment – death – for the encouragement of discipline among his own men.

The archives of Acquasparta are kept in the splendid empty Palazzo Cesi in the main square: our footsteps echoed in the great bare rooms, looked after by one elderly caretaker and his wife. He told me a request for admission should really have been addressed to the Superintendent in Perugia, but he was glad that I should admire the embossed ceilings, the reception rooms with huge fireplaces, never lit, the garden with orange trees.

One paper showed that on July 10th 1849 a request was sent from the War Ordinance of Garibaldi for bread, flour, and forage to be supplied to his troops in two days' time.

'It doesn't say for how many?'

'No. But it was sent while the General was still in Terni. That shows foresight.'

'For once, no request for shoes. I am beginning to understand about shoes. My feet *squeak*.'

Garibaldi sent ahead requests for provisions of every kind far greater than he really needed. That must have caused great distress for those who supplied the requisitions. But it served to mislead the Austrians, and their consequent overestimate of the size of his forces was one of the main reasons why they were unwilling to come to grips with him. Hoffstetter believes that had the enemy pressed hard on their heels every day and night, instead of waiting – nervously – for an opportunity for a frontal engagement, the wandering Garibaldino army would have stood no chance.

By this time there were only three thousand of them left, including Forbes's reinforcements. That was more than enough to cow any city and to procure necessary supplies. But it was very doubtful whether, even at this stage of the march, they were in any condition to fight a pitched battle. The 450 cavalry used to great effect in reconnaissance, feints and foraging, did not constitute a fighting force in Hoffstetter's opinion.

The country around Acquasparta is open and rolling, and I can understand that Garibaldi may well have thought it safer to disperse his forces until they could all reach the strongpoint of Todi. The main body appears to have taken the ridge road, marked on the Austrian map of the period, through Casteltodino. It was up to this road that we would walk on the following morning from the tiny halt of Montecastrillo, the train stopping at our request. The small, scattered villages and farmsteads hereabouts, the clumps of trees on knolls, the low-steepled churches crouching on the ridge, the scudding clouds momentarily brought to mind some gentler north-European landscape: Suffolk, for example.

Casteltodino itself, a small town of low houses built around a crossroads, records the passage of the General with a most handsome inscription, erected in 1911 on the eve of the Libyan war

– the citizens determined then to 'beautify these walls which saluted him, with a memory in marble'.

'I like lapidary Italian.'

'Just the sort of old–fashioned taste you would have.'

The art, as with the language of tombstones or of obituaries, is to imagine what the eulogy conceals. I cannot read the high-sounding tributes to Garibaldi in honour of his passage without thinking on the one hand of the flowers which were brought to him, the bands of musicians which came out to escort him: and on the other of the desperate anxiety to see him on his way as soon as possible, to keep expense to a minimum, not to incur his terrible, legendary wrath.

We walked on from Casteltodino between fields of young wheat, on the old road that switchbacked once or twice, then turned into a cattle-track which led down into the valley of the Naia. Somewhere near here, Hoffstetter watered his horse in a streamlet before which the General dismounted too, and they discovered they had 'lost' the cavalry, Hoffstetter thinking they should already have arrived in Todi and the General, correctly, saying they were still in the rear. Soon after there was a moment when Garibaldi almost lost his customary calm, and was seen galloping up the steep streets of Todi, on learning that 100 Austrian horse were expected any moment in the city. Perhaps a reconnaissance? Perhaps an advance guard? Who knew?

Hoffstetter never attempts to conceal his admiration for the character and comportment of the General – his iron calm, the evenness of his temper, the balance between Italian liveliness and American imperturbability. It was remarkable how, although anyone might have supposed that the circumstances of the Retreat would lead to familiarity between the General and his officers, even his oldest companions-in-arms who had fought with him in Uruguay would approach him with the greatest respect and consider themselves honoured should the General address them in words of friendship. Not once did he see an order of his questioned, let alone disobeyed.

'Very much the English idea of a leader of men.'

'Hoffstetter says more than once *"è nato per comandare"*.'

We were climbing up from the bridge over the Naia. Nearing Todi, we came in sight of its church tower partially concealed by the ivy-covered walls and pinnacles of a castle – a lost château or domain – before which stretched a parkland dotted with ancient mulberry trees. Exploring its deserted courtyards and looking into its empty stables, we could see no sign of present habitation except one small window open, very high up; and a few children's toys in the tall grass of the garden, by a crumbling sundial.

'Perfectly respectable quarters for the General and his lost cavalry.'

'He preferred bashing up monks.'

{VII}
Todi
(11-13 July)

W HILE FORBES'S MEN GUARDED THE GATES OF TODI, and patrolled the ground as far as the encircling Tiber, the First Legion of tired soldiers, who had marched all the way from Rome with only one day's rest, were billeted in the monastery of Cappuccini, just east of the city. Garibaldi visited the abbot, and allowed the monks to occupy a part of this monastery, and church services to continue to be held; posted guards to prevent their gardens from being trampled upon, their orchard ransacked; and arranged for a pavilion of straw to be erected for Anita. Here the ladies of Todi were to pay their respects to her for the next day or two, and satisfy their curiosity.

The convent was the scene of a great feast, a splendid surprise. A convoy of food, intended for the French commissariat in Rome, was stopped by patrols on the road to Viterbo and declared a prize of war. No fewer than 5000 birds of various kinds, and 50,000 eggs were taken. Hoffstetter describes the scene.

'Joy! Everyone wanted to have a roast, and a fry. The kitchens of the monastery smoked continuously; even so, when we left, the soldiers all carried round their necks a small bag of eggs. The monks were all the happier to cook for us as they helped in the eating, too. But with such rich food, wine was a very pleasing accompaniment, so that they had to keep on going back to the cellars again and again which rather spoilt their satisfaction.'

'Well, it won't spoil the satisfaction of the Umbria if we have another bottle.'

'You think the Spaghetti alla Boscaiola deserves it?'

We were eating in the Umbria's, terraced restaurant, overlooking the green hills and valleys. The spaghetti was cooked in a cauldron over the log fire in the great chimney. If Garibaldi's men had enjoyed the best meal of their march in Todi, that was good enough excuse for us to follow suit. Fat men dining alone are always a good sign, and the Umbria had its fair share of them. It deserves the star which it has had for many years in the Italian *Guide Michelin*. Hoffstetter – and Forbes – would have approved.

After *his* dinner, Garibaldi gathered some of his officers and men in a family circle round Anita's pavilion, and sat telling stories late into the night, until the rain came. Hoffstetter then thought he would enjoy a good night's rest on a mattress, but quickly found out that he was no longer used to such things: so went to sleep in the fresh air of the monastery passages, on the furs and cloaks he carried on each of his three horses, 'which make the most enviable of beds'.

The monastery of the Cappuccini no longer stands. But next morning we walked to Montesanto, on the small hillock between Todi and the Tiber, where some of the cavalry were quartered. The Franciscan monk who greeted us in the cloisters, showed immense good humour as he read the pages on the Feast. Their name for Garibaldi was – and is – *mangiaprete* or priest-eater; in return for one of his many uncomplimentary nicknames for them 'bread-eaters', that is to imply, idle gluttons.

Leading us towards the chapel the brother suggested that in this spot we would do better to be interested in the local saint, poet and mystic, Jacopone da Todi, whose remains were disinterred in the monastery in 1433. He had died ten years after St Francis on a Christmas Eve, the last rites administered to him by John of Verna, whom he had seen, from his tiny cell window, coming across the cold plains to his hermitage.

'I'm afraid Garibaldi did bash up monks, as you would say.'

'Forbes sounds as if he were even more bovver.'

Right or wrong, the monks everywhere were alarmed. There is one tale of shots being fired from monastery windows on a cavalry patrol returning from Foligno to Todi, killing their captain. Another savage tale illustrates the mutual enmity. An officer in charge of the rearguard presented himself at a monastery about eight miles from Todi, and asked for bread. Told that none had been baked that day, he refused to believe it. How could a monastery have no bread at all? After several requests and refusals, he intruded further, and came to a room where he saw an oven. A door opened, a monk appeared with two enormous mastiffs and one of them hurled itself at the officer. Hearing the shouts and scuffles, a soldier rushed in and shot the dog dead. The monk was unleashing the other one when more soldiers rushed in and he was saved from a lynching only by command of the wounded officer.

'A good scene.'

'The room which the monk and the dogs came out of had enough bread hidden, behind furniture, for one hundred men.'

We were walking back up the steep hill to Todi, in order to climb the church tower of San Fortunato, the highest point of the city, from where Garibaldi could see with his binoculars the Austrian positions towards Perugia. I was trying to work out the value of the fine imposed on the monastery of the mastiffs. It was 160 scudi. The salaries of some senior judges was 50 scudi a month. That might be one method. Perhaps a better one might be to relate it to the cost of horses. From the evidence of the Terni archives 160 scudi would have hired about 500 horses for a day.

'Which would cost how much nowadays?'

'I suppose say £2000 in these parts.'

The fine does not seem grossly exorbitant, especially as the offending monk was released after a few days. But there is something sad (ironic, I don't know) about this wandering Embodiment of the Roman Republic, imposing a fine upon a community whose head was also in exile – the Rome of the Popes and the Rome of the People both, for the time being, cast down, and under the yoke of a foreigner whom neither the General nor Pio Nono, for their very different reasons, welcomed in the least. *Povera Italia!*

I gave up counting the steps to the top of the bell tower of San Fortunato. The view from each arched embrasure grew more dizzying, so that the snows on the distant peaks of the Abruzzi, hard and glittering, served at each return to the eastern point of the compass, to reassure me. They at least were not hundreds of feet below, and they were constant.

At the top, underneath the great bell, I was absurdly scared at the slant of the broken flagstones. So steep was their gradient that I feared, if I added my weight by standing on the lower side of the tower, the whole edifice would tumble.

'You wouldn't do well at Pisa at all.'

'Vertigo gets worse in middle age. Wait and see.'

From the top of the tower the woods towards Perugia were visible, as they were to the General and his staff. Garibaldi sent out

forays in this and other directions; to take prisoners, gather
intelligence, and confuse the enemy about his intentions and the
size of his force. Major Migliazzi with his troop of cavalry was
already at Spoleto, and had descended on an advance post of
Austrians at Foligno, putting them to rout.

Before the forays left, the General addressed them, emphasizing
that their only security lay in constant movement: they were never
to spend the entire night in one place. They should keep in touch
with the main body through three platoons of cavalry, each of six
horses, who would ride to and fro, bringing back both news and
prisoners. All would assemble in a few days' time at Cetona, in
Tuscany.

His strike westwards from Todi remains something of a puzzle.
On the one hand there are stories of his having received letters
which gave him grounds for hope that the Tuscans were already
repenting of the restoration of their Grand Duke, and were ripe for
another revolution. On the other hand Hoffstetter insists that his
whole strategy was unchanged: that is, to reach the coast at the best
possible point for embarkation to Venice, with as much of his army
as possible intact.

Otherwise, so he argues, if Garibaldi had any serious confidence
in a Tuscan insurrection, why not press on? Why linger in Todi?
Why leave Forbes's cannon and stores of ammunition here?
Alternatively, if he wanted to make a stand here in the
subapeninnes, why not seize the opportunity to attack the Austrians
while many of their units were isolated?

'I am dizzy with the calculation.'

'Serves you right for being an amateur strategist on the top of a
church.'

But bell towers from which you can point to far grounds and
middle grounds and trace contours, and shade your eyes with a
hand, are good places for such amateurs: at least, if they do not
suffer from vertigo.

The broad road from Todi to Orvieto, seen winding from our
vantage point as in the background of a Renaissance painting, now
follows the banks of the Tiber and the shores of the newly-dammed
Lake Corbara. But this did not exist in 1849. Indeed, no proper
road at all ran between the two cities, only a bridle-path. Two or
three miles downhill from Todi and after crossing the Ponte Acuto,
the ancient bridge whose sharp spurs jut out into the yellow water

like the bows of a ship, the old road zigzags up and up: 365 curves, it is said, into bare hills.

Garibaldi had left Todi because he did not wish to be trapped in the city; and made his midday halt at the Carthusian monastery, probably the one of the mastiffs, where they obtained cheese, salami and wine without much ceremony.

'That would explain the reception which the officer in charge of the rearguard got.'

'But when the monks complained, they got a thump on the head.'

They left the monastery for their evening march at about four o'clock. There was some trouble getting the troops to start, because too much food and wine had made them sleepy. It was a hard march, too. Hoffstetter says:

'Our road was nothing but a mountain path, narrow, rocky and steep. The Signora of the General rode at the head of the column which stretched for miles, since it was possible to march only in single file. We had no water until the village of Prodo, but at least enjoyed magnificent views over Tuscany and into Romagna, marching as we did on the ridge of the mountains.'

Magnificent indeed! These sombre uplands are wonderful for walking today: moorland country almost as remote and desolate as the Highlands of Scotland, but with now and then a wayside chapel or shrine, now and then a long avenue of trees leading to a farmstead. We saw a few animals: two hares, some horses, a flock of sheep; the sky hung low.

By leaving Todi on the one bus of the day, at six o'clock, and asking to be set down not too far from Prodo, we were able, even though breakfastless, to enjoy the solitude of these hills, the rising sun behind us illuminating the western plateaux towards Viterbo, mists in the valleys beneath us, like lakes of milk, dissolving. Hoffstetter calls Prodo a miserable village. True, it is too high for olives and vines, and in winter the winds must be bitter, but it is today a trim village of one street, and the lawns before the gaunt fortress on its westward side are close-cropped by sheep. At seven the café was opened, and one old man, proud to boast that he was to be eighty-five next birthday, served coffee to us, his only customers.

'Ask him about Garibaldi.'

'Unkind, so early in the morning.'

But hesitantly, searching in his memory, he recounted how, indeed, his grandfather had sat him on his knee when he was tiny and told him of the time when *he* had been the same age, and was awoken by the clinking and clanking of bridles, as the army made its way towards the great hollow just beyond the village, where they camped. Here, at last, they found water which falls in crystal leaps into a cirque – 'a spring that gave us the best water possible'. In this hollow they thought themselves concealed well enough to take the risk of lighting fires for cooking. This was where Anita had her tent pitched on a rocky spur, and where she laid out a supper of leftovers, of which they kept back the best part for the General. For Garibaldi had stayed behind at Todi and Anita was torn between fear that he might be riding at night over heights and along paths which were dangerous enough by day – and hope that he would not, for all that, wait till dawn to leave Todi. How glad she was to see him arrive an hour before midnight!

As we circled this hollow, there beneath us in a vegetable patch near an old, grey stone bridge, stood a scarecrow in a Garibaldi-red shirt, wearing a beret in which was planted a scraggy feather.

'Too good to be true.'

'But not worn *alla calabrese*. And *certainly* not an ostrich feather.'

'Enough to frighten the birds, if no one else.'

Garibaldi did not enjoy frightening the peasants at all. Let Hoffstetter tell the tale, '. . . in these solitary fastnesses the shepherds with their flocks took to their heels so soon as they saw us. But one of them, who probably hadn't seen us, suddenly found himself forty steps away. He didn't want to stop at my summons, and since rocks and landslips prevented my following him, I pointed my pistol at him. The General begged me not to frighten the poor runaway, and by a few words of friendship at last persuaded him to come near. One or two questions, and this man became so trusting that he offered to be our guide. Reassured, a few other shepherds came up to satisfy their curiosity. How well the General knew how to handle these people and always bring out the best in them! In a few minutes they outbid each other in forthcomingness, telling us all that they knew of the enemy and of his plans. Often, on occasions like this I heard the General say "Why be afraid? Do we speak German? Do we exact money by threatening to set fire to your homes? Are we assassins? Do we fight for you or against you? Are we not fellow-countrymen?"'

I suppose it is not unusual to find courtesy and gentleness towards others dwelling in the same character side by side with severity and harshness towards one's own. At Prodo a soldier was caught stealing a hen, and summarily executed. At the noise of the gunshots the General rose and addressed the troops, who did not know what was happening, and were understandably startled, 'That is how I punish thieves! Are we murderers, or do we fight for liberty? Are we here to defend the people, or to oppress them?'

'There's a suggestion of wild see-saws in Garibaldi's behaviour, all the same.'

'I think what you're trying to say is that he suffered from hypermania. Over-active. Not like you, dear father.'

In any case, the soldiers very wisely shouted *'viva Garibaldi'* when their comrade was shot and, so Hoffstetter says, the ones who shouted the loudest were those who were chewing on the stolen hen.

Amidst this cajoling and chastising, the General found time, before leaving Prodo at noon, to write a letter to the Chief Magistrate at Orvieto in which he requested rations for 4000 men, and forage for 600 horses. He said that he proposed to camp outside the city walls, just before the bridge over the Paglia. This letter, a copy of which is in the Orvieto archives, casts a strange light on the silent fury he showed later, when told that the gates of Orvieto were shut against him.

'But he could still have been cross. Very annoying to have gates slammed in your face.'

'Cross is an understatement. He even threatened to wheel up his old cannon.'

This was now the only piece of artillery they had with them, Forbes's two field-guns having been left behind in Todi. The paths along which they now struggled were so precipitous that sometimes it had to be dismounted, detached from the four horses which drew it, and manhandled – not a job for a July afternoon.

Some of the short-cuts which we took led up and down such steep and intractable paths, often interrupted by landslides and overgrown with thorn hedges under which we crawled. Once or twice, bent double, we glimpsed valleys far beneath the sudden, dangerous precipices whose edge we had reached unawares.

Towards noon we were rewarded by our first view of Orvieto, still a long way below us, the sheer cliff on which it is built bathed in sunlight: a toy city at this distance, round and compact, with battlements that reminded me of some medieval wood-engraving of a Greek or Roman siege – easy to conjure up battering-rams, ladders, chunky, breastplated centurions.

Doubtful tracks led off across moorland, and plunged down through scrub-oaks, into ravines. In England, even in Scotland, it is easy to come down from mountains; but in the Apennines often I have found myself struggling in gorges through almost impenetrable thickets, having descended into the wrong valley, or system of valleys. Yet it is feeble to follow the gentle gradients of roads made for cars. And once this morning we saved at least one steep mile, aided by a beckoning line of cypresses: the church tower at the end – the lower end – reassuringly in line with the sun-yellow turrets of Orvieto.

'What was the first the city knew of the approach of the horde, do you imagine?'

'That Prodo letter, obviously.'

But no! On July 8th the Chief Magistrate of Todi wrote to his counterpart at Orvieto that press reports told of Garibaldi heading towards his city with an army of no fewer than 12,000 men. Surely almost a relief to learn that they were asked to provide food for 5000 at most? Not that anyone knew where this army was heading. Ruggieri, fellow-marcher with Hoffstetter, wrote of this stage, 'The Austrians began to show signs of life. Learning of the march of Garibaldi on Todi, which was contrary to all their calculations, they reduced their garrisons in Ancona and other Adriatic cities, and increased those of Umbria, to put themselves in a position to contest a march on Perugia towards the legations (i.e. Emilia, Romagna, Bologna) . . . In a word, General Aspre from Florence, and General Gorzkowski from Bologna prepared to put their heavy forces into the field: the one against any advance of Garibaldi into Tuscany, the other to prevent any attempt of his to stir the already fermenting revolt in Romagna.'

So Garibaldi's strategy – if indeed this is not mere hindsight – of drawing his enemies after him, thereby to open up an escape path across the Apennines to a port in the Upper Adriatic, could be said to be working.

Meanwhile, viewed from these heights, the courage (or bravado) of sending out patrols in all directions into these wild, high regions in order to bluff both Austrians and French, commands amazed respect. Patrols subtracted from an attenuated force, dwindling every day with desertions!

Orvieto
(14-15 July)

THE ARCHIVES OF ORVIETO are housed in a cloister, noisy with schoolchildren – one large room leading off a dark corridor. Here the staff had been extraordinarily kind and assiduous in searching out, in response to the standard letter I sent in advance, all the documents relating to 1849, fascicle after dusty fascicle.

It is time, after having spent so long in the company of the Swiss Major, to present another side of the story, and to show how the ruling citizens of a town saw those days when they were the unwilling and fearful hosts to the General and his army.

Here then, is how these citizens referred back to the Council who had appointed them to compose the official account.

'. . . You had hardly returned home from the Council meeting on Friday July 13 when we had news of ten lancers of Garibaldi arriving at the Porta Cassia. The fierce reputation of the General, the treatment that Todi had suffered, the scant discipline of his troops, all gave your committee grounds for extreme apprehension, and so, instead of welcoming them at once into the city, we resolved to go to the gate to hear their intentions, to inspect their posts, and only then to decide what action to take. On the mission you yourselves were witnesses of the excited temper of our citizens, and especially of the countrypeople, who nearly came to blows. Therefore our resolution was unanimous, and with the most courteous expressions we invited the lancers to return to the hostelry at Paglia, promising to send down to them someone who would listen to their requests, and treat with them. On our return to the commune we learnt from a scout sent to Todi that Garibaldi with his main body of about 4000 men was approaching Prodo, and on this news anyone who knows anything of the mood of our city, will easily appreciate that the only course which lay open to us was that of appeasement. We wrote to the leader of the platoon to inquire what refreshments he had need of. Later, with a rare example of self-sacrifice and patriotism our Colonel Ravizza (and others) formed a deputation to go to the bridge. No longer 10 but nearer 100 Garibaldini were there. They demanded provisions, lodging, twenty-four crowns in cash and twenty-three crowns in coupons. All this was sent to them at once and the deputation left them fully satisfied.

'To show the temper of the city we need only mention that during the day a few citizens, or rather labourers, tried to riot; and in the evening some of our youth asked to go to the Paglia bridge. Permission was refused them and . . . the precaution, already decided in Council the previous day, of reinforcing the guards of the gates, was put into effect.

'On Saturday morning, our Adjutant-Major came hurriedly to tell us that an aide-de-camp of Garibaldi, with several soldiers, was at the gate, and threatening to enter at all costs. Confronted with this escalation, three of your Committee went to speak to them: a chink was carefully opened in the gate, and conversation began. We found ourselves talking to Pietro Stagnetti, our fellow-citizen. We took heart from this. His arrival seemed a sure sign that Garibaldi's intentions were not hostile. The closing of the gates on the previous day was discussed. Furious at first, he ended by accepting our arguments, and requested provisions: 4500 rations of bread, wine and salted meat [evidently they were hoping for a change from their South American diet] and provender for 500 horse. We sent out as much as we could collect on the spot. When he came to talk of money he demanded the terrifying sum of 30,000 crowns.* However, he stated that this could be reduced to the – scarcely less exorbitant – sum of 10,000 crowns. We took him to the Commune and tried to make him amenable. We presented him with a sword. But perhaps all this would have come to nothing had not . . . his brother and brother-in-law added their urgent entreaties. It took several hours, but the requisition was at last reduced to 2000 crowns, in silver. All the good citizens of the country, including those who had left the city but not abandoned it altogether, volunteered to help . . . and by evening the sum had been collected.

'Midday had just passed when either through our guards' carelessness or cowardice some lancers managed to enter the city. Stagnetti sent them back immediately to their camp, together with

* I estimate this at roughly the equivalent of £900,000 in today's terms – for a city of 9000 souls.

the provisions which they said they had come to get. But the terror which their entry inspired was as nothing compared to that created later by Stagnetti himself when he returned from the camp to announce that . . . the General himself, with a few of his escort, had gone to the Porta Cassia and to the Porta Portuga and, finding them closed, had returned, threatening, taciturn, ordering his men outside the gates to cut down poplars and prepare ladders.

'Gentlemen, in such a crisis what could we do? It would have been wilful folly to expose our citizenry to extreme dangers, by attempting to resist a force of about 4000 armed men determined to carry forward any desperate undertaking. Our choice therefore was simply whether to have the General as friend or as foe – since have him we must.

'Your committee of three went out to him in a deputation . . . We found him at first haughty, but after we had explained our reasons for shutting the gates his manner became very courteous. We invited him to come up into the city, begging him to leave his men behind. He accepted and promised that not a single soldier would come up, without his express orders. In fact his wife and a few aides-de-camp accompanied and followed him. His reception in the Commune was honest, and he willingly granted that no mass be celebrated for his force in the Cathedral – as several of his followers had proposed. Moreover, he wrote a note in which he forbade the remainder of his army to enter the city, and cause further damage.

'In the light of this can you imagine our surprise when in the morning we saw the streets of the city crowded with fully-armed men, going about both singly and in ordered patrols? And our dismay too, at their threatening manners, the continual coming and going of their officers into the Commune, where they made the most extravagant demands? To begin with we put up some resistance, but when Gianuzzi (the officer into whose hands we had paid over 2000 crowns on Saturday) . . . made the formal request for 700 pairs of shoes, several horses and shirts, and gave us coupons in exchange, assuring us of their validity, what could we do at the head of a city in their hands? The lesser evil was to agree . . .

'The communal chest emptied and – even worse – the Convent of S. Domenico pillaged, are facts which clearly show the ideas these men entertained and which we hope will justify our yielding for the sake of the whole city.

'About ten o'clock in the evening a messenger brought us news of the approach of the French who, before entering the city, sent a request that it should be illuminated. The Council received the incomers to the applause of many of the people – as you already know – and very soon the men were quartered under cover and provender supplied for their horses.'

If this was by far the most comprehensive of the papers of the day, there were many other pieces for us to thumb through, in the grey light of that bare tall-ceilinged room, whose silence was broken only by the occasional scissor-clip of an assistant diligently compiling, from ancient newspapers, an Orvieto scrapbook of some later period. There was Gianuzzi's receipt for the 'contribution' of 2000 crowns, so drastically reduced from 30,000; and the order signed by the Chief Magistrate to the Commander of the National Guard, bidding him to close the gates to everyone, save only to any of the troops of Garibaldi wanting to *go out*.

'Strange that none of the later historians put the Orvieto side of the case.'

'I certainly don't believe, now, that the city was lit up in his honour, as Trevelyan says.'

'Of course the Orvieto people may, cunningly, have led him to *believe* it was in his honour?'

In this connection Hoffstetter states only that Garibaldi allowed himself to be persuaded by the third deputation to enter the city, and then the dark streets of the city were suddenly illuminated as for a feast day. 'From all this,' he goes on, 'one can only conclude that what weighed most on the citizens' minds was the nuisance of having to lodge us. That wouldn't have happened anyway, while we camped outside the city. The closing of the gates could only damage the interests of the inhabitants – because the General had decided to use force.'

'I wonder if he really had?'

'He made only noises later on at Arezzo, when they kept him out. No siege, no fight in the end.'

For Garibaldi hated the idea of setting Italians to fight Italians, and may well have realized that it would do his cause no good. His threat to bring up the old cannon, and to cut down poplars for an assault by scaling the walls, would then have been bluff.

What does seem clear from the report of the Orvietan committee is that the principal reason for closing the gates was fear of civil insurrection. That seems fair justification, and one which Garibaldi appears at the time to have accepted. And the restored Papal authorities also appear to have accepted the reasons for the Council's meeting of Garibaldi's demands: a few days later a Te Deum in thanks for the city's salvation was sung in a packed Cathedral.

Not indeed, as Farini wrote of life in the Papal States, that there was ever any shortage of Te Deums. Especially, it is fair to suppose, in the magnificent cathedral of a city which claims to have been the residence of no fewer than thirty-two popes – attracted by its almost impregnable position during the thirteenth and fourteenth centuries.

Garibaldi's own memories of his visit were rose-tinted by the time he visited it again, sixteen years later. Still Rome was the temporal Dominion of the Pope and under the protection of the French. Still Garibaldi's theme was 'Without Rome . . . Italy cannot be'. He addressed the citizens, more enthusiastic this time than last, from the balcony of the Albergo Belle Arti. 'We meet again . . . after that time when certain Jesuits wished to lock the gates of the city against us. But the People claimed their due rights, and welcomed the remnants of Freedom and of the Defence of Rome.'

'You don't think he might have been made more amenable by this Orvieto wine . . . agreeable amnesia?'

'No. Perfectly reasonable rhetoric. Anyway, he was always rather abstemious.'

We had descended into one of those cellars, dripping with ancient tallow, where butts of Orvieto wine line the cave-walls. Plastic tubing hung over railings. We drank to Hoffstetter, to whose company we would return on the march next day. He had himself observed on going out of the gates a shop where 'every passer-by was offered, from butts, drinks of the friendly, restorative beverage (*l'amichevole bevanda ristorativa*)'.

This seems an admirable way to refer to Orvieto wines – indeed justifies drinking any good wine – and I am most grateful to our guide for introducing me to it.

On the eve of our next walk we climbed to the small park, dotted with umbrella pines, which lies at the upper end of the city. From here, with our hands on the railings which guard the sheer precipice of the rock, we could clearly make out the place of encampment between the two rivers, the Paglia and the Chiana. On the day

Garibaldi left, there was an outbreak of disorder – many of the troops wading across the river, eager to taste the pleasures of the city, despite the prohibition.

Garibaldi ordered departure instantly. This was a fairly effective means of bringing most of the troops to heel, but even so, it took a good two hours before mounted patrols had rounded up the recalcitrants, thumping some of them on the head. In the end, the main body was only a mile away from Orvieto, marching hurriedly in the dark, before they heard reports of the French entering the illuminated city.

From our eminence we could map out, too, the route of our next day's walk. The eye followed the course of the Chiana, as it wound down towards us in a cleft valley, covered with trees. We guessed that this might be the passage where Hoffstetter fell into a daydream. 'Our march to Ficulle passed up a long defile . . . at whose entry we were refreshed by the shade of a thick, tall hedge of oaks. I fancied myself suddenly transported to my homeland. A yearning rose in me, such as I had not felt for a long time, one which could not very often rise to the surface in the continuous noise and bustle; so that, now, I forgot altogether about the French, and jog-trotted mechanically behind the troops.'

Their march that night was silent and wary, with good reason. It was not so much the French behind them in Orvieto who now presented the threat, as the Austrians who were closing in ahead: one division three marches away in Siena, another two marches away in Perugia, and a third very near indeed at Marsciano. Towards Tuscany, into the mouth of these fierce armies, who were unrestrained by any lingering notions of 'fraternity', un-encumbered by any half-hearted or ambiguous instructions from their Government, they were now advancing.

We stared down into the clear brown eddies of the Chiana, shoals of tiny fish seeking refuge beneath flat stones. At ten o'clock in the morning, passing over the bridge of the river within yards of its junction with the Paglia, thus more or less on the site of Garibaldi's encampment – now marked out for factory development – we were at last leaving the civilized delights of Orvieto behind us after two days' most agreeable rest, spent partly in the archives, partly in the cellars.

'Which, I suppose, are also archives in their way.'

'*Well.*'

Clearly the chief purpose of our day's walk was to discover and
follow the deep, romantic defile which reminded the excellent Swiss
Major of forest paths in his homeland. This search occupied us for
the first two hours, so soon as we had left the plain and begun to
approach the hills which separated us from our destination, Ficulle.
No stream which ran down the steep hillside was too trifling to
escape a brief, hopeful examination. Suppose we followed it just a
little further up, might we not find a way between rocky crags,
climb up a tree-lined gorge? A holm-oak, about a hundred feet up,
gave me a brief, wild moment of encouragement.

'Too much to hope that the actual oaks would still be living.'

'Let's just find a narrow defile first and worry about the trees
later.'

Once or twice we left the road for stretches of a half-mile or so,
taking short-cuts through spring meadows along the banks of the
swift-flowing Chiana.

At last we came to a point where the road starts its upward loops,
and where a torrent tumbled underneath an old stone bridge down
into the Chiana, shaded by poplars. Here a path meandered away
across some scrubland before entering into the woods and half-
losing itself in brambles and thickets.

'Exactly the right direction.'

'What do you mean, the right direction?'

'Towards Ficulle.'

'But away from the Chiana. Away from the valley we saw from
Orvieto.'

Fruitless dissension! The end was amicable. We took the middle
way and walked up the steep road to the village of Bagni. True, this
was the one course which could not possibly be Hoffstetter's. But
perhaps from a little further up, and a little further up again, we
might be able to spy the elusive defile? This defile became an
obsession, like Captain Ahab's white whale.

'It's no good. We shall have to go back.'

'But I want my lunch.'

'*Lunch??* If we don't find the defile, we shall have to go back and
find it.'

At each bend in the road we peered down into possible and
impossible narrows.

'Earth-moving machines might have filled it in since 1849.'

'Nothing very like Zurich here.'

'But Hoffstetter says he went into a dream.'

'Nothing that looks like a long, oak-lined Swiss defile to me.'

We climbed up through the village of Bagni, leaving the road only to inspect a derelict octagonal hut which guarded a well: broken panes of stained glass lay on the sandy soil, vivid red and blue, on which could be made out, as in a jigsaw, a shape that looked like the dilated nostrils of a white charger. Hunger and the approach of lunch brought back to me Hoffstetter's tale of the boy Raymond who cared for his three horses.

'He looked after them extremely well, always finding provender even when others went without. On the other hand he didn't seem able to get anything for *my* table, and if I hadn't been able to share the General's meal, I should often have gone very hungry. Sometimes, though, that table was pretty meagre – a few boiled eggs and a small piece of hard cheese. I gave Raymond a lecture on the need always to have a reserve of roast chickens. One day I lost my temper when as usual he had nothing for me. To avoid any recurrence of this, and to get back into my good books, he once bought in Terni a couple of chickens and came to meet me bearing them in triumph, quite forgetting that in that city there were excellent restaurants I could go to.'

'I really don't think we should have lunch till we've identified the defile.'

'I suppose we could go on just a little further.'

We passed a billboard which announced the boundary of the region of Orvieto Classico. By this stage of Garibaldi's march the night had fallen dark and moonless on the rearguard, the only illumination being the fortress city of Orvieto, in the distance.

'Probably invisible from the defile though. Couldn't be seen through the thick hedge of oaks.'

'I wonder what sort of supper they had in Ficulle?'

Not until we were on the brow of the hill which descends into the village did we abandon our hopeless search and start upon our lunch; and even then we cast lingering looks behind us; traced with our fingers possible candidates on the map; suggested, and rejected, descents into the dry beds of torrents.

If, in the end, our obsession waned, it was due only to the excellence of our picnic, and to the late afternoon consumption of a reasonable quantity of the *amichevole bevanda ristorativa.*

Ficulle

(15-16 July)

Hoffstetter, bringing up the rear, rode down into the small hillside town of Ficulle late on the evening of July 15th; and he counted himself very lucky to find, at midnight, some of the rice prepared by Anita for the General, left over and still warm. The troops had made their way through a gap in the thick hedge of thorn trees, lit by flares, into a meadow where they camped near a fountain. The thorn trees are no more, but the fountain, falling into two great stone troughs, still flows abundantly at all seasons of the year; and Ficulle's only hotel, where we stayed, is built nearby.

Poor Hoffstetter! That night he must have had less than two hours' sleep, for at one-thirty he was up again to call the men to arms, after a most uncomfortable rest in which he was soaked by a heavy dew. And then at dawn, while the rations were being cooked, he was off on a reconnaissance, looking back towards Orvieto: both reassured, and a little surprised, to find no evidence of any pursuit by the French. In the light of all this activity it is not surprising that his memories of this stop are scant.

Many years later Belluzzi, the school inspector of Bologna and devoted student and chronicler of the Retreat, was lucky to discover an old man of Ficulle who could remember a great deal about the passage of Garibaldi. Signor Bracchetti had bought some land from the Convent of the Sisters of St Paul and, a year after Garibaldi's death, erected a small monument in the olive grove where Anita and her husband had pitched their tent, underneath the split trunk of an ancient tree – alas no longer standing – which had furcated so much that it appeared at first sight to form five separate trees.

'Doesn't he say he unveiled the monument on the same day as the Ficulle Society of Clay Pigeon Shooters was founded?'

'Garibaldi was an acceptable hero to the bourgeois by the time he was as old as you.'

Certainly some commemoration is to take place on the anniversary of Garibaldi's death in 1982. Signor Bracchetti particularly remembered Garibaldi's two-hour inspection of the camp, and his insistence that the horses had all the provender they needed. Only after this did he pay his respects to the local authorities and demand a 'tax' of 3000 crowns, reduced in the end to 345.

That seems to have been the custom at this stage of the Retreat: to ask for about ten times the sum eventually agreed. Ficulle, a much smaller town than Orvieto, was unlucky to have had to pay up the equivalent of some £10,000. However, memories of the exaction had faded, and turned into a rosier sense of having been honoured, by the time of Garibaldi's death. The plaque of 1885:

> The glorious remnants of the Roman Republic
> Having escaped from the fratricidal French
> Republic – Giuseppe Garibaldi passed by
> Here with them and was fêted on July 15 1849 . . .

'Extraordinary how the Italians put their trust in the French!'
'Always a mistake.'
We were looking up at the inscription on the town hall. It was very early on the morning of Easter Sunday, and we had been woken by bells, which echoed across the high valleys.

The French, fratricides though they may well be thought, had now ceased to pursue Garibaldi, despite a letter written on July 22nd by General Oudinot in Rome to the Austrian General D'Aspre in Florence.

'The French flying column under the orders of General Morris has pursued the troops of Garibaldi to the utmost. The partisan leader seems to have ceased to burden the Roman States, yet our mission will not be completed until the bands which he commands have been totally dispersed.'

Yet the French were not to move any further at all, in fact.
'Garibaldi wasn't to know that though.'
'That remains a mystery.'
Could it be due to all the press reports that his army was 12,000 strong? *Surely* the French intelligence was better than that! Belluzzi thinks that such reports provided the excuse, and that what really lay behind the French irresolution, their total failure to come to grips with Garibaldi, was the desire to leave the dirty work to the

Austrians, and to the Tuscan Grand Duke who had called their divisions to their aid. Let *them* bear the odium!

'And what do you make of Garibaldi being fêted here?'

'Hospitality was always the best way to get rid of him.'

But possibly we were being unfair to Ficulle's generosity, for Belluzzi tells how at least one inhabitant opened up his cellars, and sent out wine to the troops, in barrelfuls. That was something to be remembered.

There were memories, too, in Ficulle of the General's patience in listening to the beseechings of a peasant, who threw himself on his knees before him, and told him a sad tale of damage done to some property belonging to the Chapter: and of how his reverend masters had refused to accept his excuse and let him off, so that he – poor, miserable peasant that he was – would have to bear all the cost. At the end of his story (but not till then?) Garibaldi made him rise to his feet, and promised that all damage would be made good, and sent him off with 'something to buy a drink with'.

Belluzzi adds, with a note of piety pleasingly absent from Hoffstetter's tales, that 'it was particularly interesting, and shows the suffering as well as the courage of the Hero, that while the General was listening to the peasant's tale, he was removing some bandages, soaked with grease, and drying his feet which were bloody and wounded; yet no word of complaint or swearing escaped his lips.'

'We must find the stone bench now, outside Signor Bracchetti's front door.'

'Too early in the morning to bother.'

It was indeed early on the morning of July 16th that Garibaldi went to inspect both camps, one of infantry near the fountain, enclosed in the thick thorn hedge: and the other of cavalry, in a convent on the other side of the town. On his way between the two he stopped in the street and sat down on a stone seat and addressed the boys who swarmed round him. 'In your time, *Italianini*, you must fight to free your country.' Belluzzi adds that he laid great weight on the last words. Surely to have spoken thus to a group of village children was, in his desperate situation, not rhetoric meant for the world but an act of faith?

'Belluzzi always makes the General sound unbearably noble.'

'He woke everyone up too early, so he must have been.'

We walked out of Ficulle, up a winding road towards the

monastery of the Cappuccini in whose grounds the cavalry had stayed. Here at least there was no doubt that we had found the correct spot. High walls encompass an orchard, and the peace, proper to a monastery, is preserved in the atmosphere of what is now an old people's home: one which, to the passer-by at least, seems both serene and orderly: the courtyard trim, a small patch of herbs fragrant in one corner.

On each side of the road along which we walked, olives grew at grotesque angles out of the high ground, many of them ancient and furcated like the tree under which the General slept, so that it was easy to see how Anita and her pages might have covered the wizened stems with the tent which she had so diligently been sewing: difficult only to imagine how the trees themselves continued to live – especially, to an untrained eye, during these Easter days when the pruners go to their work so savagely that it seems only dead branches point out at the sky, green loppings scattered everywhere in the avenues.

The up-and-down way was steep but by mid-morning we had reached the escarpment overlooking the valley of the Grand Canal of the Chiana, which stretches as flat as fenland for twenty-five miles northwards. The only question was how we should descend. Short-cuts beckoned us, and we walked down and round edges of fields, before plunging into trackless woods and thickets of scrub-oak.

We scrambled precipitously down, clutching less expertly than Tarzan on to trailing ropes of Traveller's Joy and of ivy, stumbled into dells made soft by leaf-mould, were torn by brambles and yet enticed ever onwards by the sound of falling water. Any stream must lead us sooner or later to a junction with the Chiana, to navigable paths. So thick was the panoply of green above us that, half-closing my eyes, I could transport myself into a jungle. Nor was this over-fanciful. For soon we were clambering down the rocky bed of a torrent – a defile far, far narrower than any Hoffstetter could have trotted along – until we emerged into a level clearing, treacherous with stagnant ponds and bog-asphodel. Here the stream mysteriously divagated, dribbled away. Ankle-deep, and with some fear, we skirted the quagmire. At the far end we were stopped by a most unexpected obstacle: tumbles of stone and a vast, neglected system of weirs. Were these the ruins of some mill abandoned civilizations ago? Gingerly we walked across one mossy boulder, gazing down no more than a hundred feet (but that was quite enough) into a gorge, fed by trickles and seepings through the forgotten, useless dam.

We slithered down some slime-covered stones and stood in a bed of waist-high nettles.

'I don't think I like your short-cuts.'

'Any more than Garibaldi's donkey did?'

It was not far from here, on a night of torrential downpour, that one of the poor donkeys, loaded with guns, fell exhausted into a ditch and became hopelessly entangled in the cords of its harness. It brayed so demonically that the sound could be heard for miles, betraying their position, so it was feared, to the French who Garibaldi thought were hard on his heels.

We ourselves stood at last on the bridge over the Chiana at Carnaiuola: and looked down into the slow-moving waters of what looks more like a drainage canal than a river. It was hard to tell which way it was flowing. Surely not eastwards, towards the mountains? Surely westwards and northwards along the flat plain?

'Hoffstetter says Garibaldi marched up the *left* bank for two hours.'

'Which *is* the left bank?'

Our confusion was pardonable. All this long, dead-level stretch in the centre of Italy, could once be made to drain either north into the Arno, or south into the Tiber. Malaria-ridden marshland in the Middle Ages, only in the last century – twenty years after Garibaldi had criss-crossed its dykes and canals – was the Val di Chiana fully reclaimed, and its waters finally sent south.

After he had crossed the bridge where we were standing Garibaldi surprised everyone by suddenly turning west. They were not after all going to pass through Città di Pieve. His scouts had told him that the Tuscan garrison had closed the gates against him, expecting Austrian reinforcements from Perugia. Guided by a succession of men, not very willingly, his army floundered across the wet, difficult terrain, many of the horses stumbling into ditches as their riders dozed. Some of the infantry almost fainted from thirst, and Hoffstetter knocked up an isolated farmhouse to ask for water.

'The wretched, terrified inhabitants begged us to wait till they were dressed, hoping perhaps that we would be impatient and go away. I was really more out of temper with the soldiers than with

Ficulle (15-16 July)

the householders . . . "SILENCE" I shouted, "go quickly, take some hay and set alight to this hovel! If they won't give you water, let them pay the price." The doors were opened at once, and a man appeared fully-dressed, excusing himself on the grounds that he couldn't find his trousers. He was trembling all over, and begged for mercy. "Fool! Beast!" the soldiers yelled at him. "All we want is water. We have the devil of a thirst. Fetch us water." The man was so relieved that he wanted to bring wine, too – but the soldiers refused it.'

'The only recorded instance of Hoffstetter refusing wine.'

'Stupid idiot.'

Our scramble down through the thickets, our difficult negotiation of the morass by the forgotten weir, had seriously delayed us, and by the time we arrived at the railway halt of Fabbro, just beyond the Carnaiuola bridge, lunch was no longer to be found. All we had for Easter celebration was a piece of dry sponge cake. Whether it was this, or the flatness of the land over which we now made our way – bleak, neglected-looking farmhouses scattered here and there in a network of ditches – our mood was not so exhilarated as it should have been on the Day of Resurrection. There was also the question where we should stay that night. Enquiries had not been hopeful. Salci, near which our hero camped, was said to be unlikely to be able to provide beds.

The noise of the Florence–Rome motorway, under which we were to walk, grew in our ears. Just before it, down a half-finished track, there stood what was probably a hotel, even though the billboard was lying on the ground. Ancient farm-carts, half-restored, stood near its entrance. Iron lanterns were affixed to doorposts.

'I'm not sure if I trust *cartwheels* outside hotels. Especially hotels by motorways.'

'There's nowhere else. I told you you should have looked.'

Restored, in a style designed to resemble that of a smallish monastery, rooms facing inwards on to a cloister at whose grassy centre a wrought-iron well-head was being built, this hotel, all but finished at the time of our brief stay, might well sound as if it were the equivalent of some oak-beamed roadhouse of the Home Counties. Yet it wasn't like that, somehow. True, the collection of farm-carts, painted in Sicilian blue and orange, could not be counted as authentic decoration. But, walking round the outer

81

battlements of the building, we sometimes opened a door on to a jumble of high-backed chairs, or odd pieces of plumbing-to-be. And we rested our feet in cool, paved reception rooms, intended for motorists rather than walkers. We appeared to be almost the only guests. No service could have been more solicitous.

Several yards away in one direction the noise of the motorway was muffled. Several yards in another direction, I was delighted by the apparition, well and alive and *not* collapsed into a ditch, of a donkey outside the arches, ears laid back, but not braying.

Cetona
(17-18 July)

EARLY ON THE MORNING OF EASTER MONDAY, we set off
on one of our longest walks, thirty kilometres across hills and
valleys to Cetona. The sky was light blue, with fleecy clouds, the air
crisp – impossible to imagine a greater contrast with the dark July
night of deluge on which Garibaldi and his dwindling band started
upon the same march. Villas set upon hilltops, their gardens
surrounded by trees, announced the approach of the gentler, more
civilized countryside of Tuscany.

The white, unpaved road led downhill to a bridge over the
Torrente Argento, suitably named since its water was clear and
silvery in the sunlight. This was perhaps the stream up whose
northern bank Garibaldi had marched for two hours, before
crossing it and marching back again.

'As bad as the Duke of Plaza Toro.'

'Are you sure you don't mean the Grand Old Duke of York?'

By manoeuvres such as these he deceived D'Aspre into sending
one contingent from Florence to Siena, and another force to
Livorno which prepared to embark for Porto Santo Stefano. A
number of American ships had gathered in these waters in order, so
the Austrian General believed, to aid Garibaldi's escape.

As we approached Salci, a castle rose in the air above us,
pinnacled, turreted, surrounded by great pines which the winds had
buffeted to stand at all angles. But an air of desolation sat upon it;
windows were boarded up, outbuildings had lost their roofs, fences
lay broken on the ground.

'Fairy castles should be desolate. At the most, a prisoner in the
top turret.'

'Wouldn't be a bad idea if they locked you up.'

Two minutes later we were walking underneath an arch, and
entered the tiny village of Salci, a single rectangle of uniform houses

facing inwards into a courtyard bright with spring flowers. The arch of the gateway on the other side framed a view of a fertile valley, across whose wooded head ran the borders of Tuscany. Seeing us point and stare and take photographs, a priest ambled towards us, happy to tell the tale of the castle, and of the family who for six hundred years, in an unbroken line, had owned the domain of almost 10,000 acres. After the unification of Italy, and the final demise of the sovereignty of the Pope over Rome, there were quarrels over the succession: all troubles in Italy, he said, sprung from this date. It seemed unpropitious, in the circumstances, to ask for any local recollection of Garibaldi the priest-eater.

It was upon entering Tuscany that Hoffstetter made some unflattering observations about the way a regime of priests makes a population decadent. In the Papal States the local inhabitants had usually fled at the sight of the column, or stared at the soldiers dumbly. But now 'the Tuscans came forward to meet us with jubilation, bringing up wine as we marched along the roads, everyone volunteering to be our guide. In short, we were made thoroughly welcome.'

His mood was lifted, too, by the glorious day which followed a night of continuous rain which had drenched them all 'to the marrow-bone', and the smiling countryside had never looked more beautiful. For the first time his soldiers believed they might be advancing, not retreating. But well received though they may have been, they were still in a land whose government, local and central, was hostile to revolutionaries. The Grand Duke was about to return to the acclamation of his subjects.

It is true that the loyal efforts made for his restoration by all the Tuscan cities (save Livorno) had been soured by the Austrian General D'Aspre, who had entered Florence on May 25th at the head of 9000 men, to the sound of military bands; and had issued a proclamation that 'Austria has decided to yield to the wishes of . . . the Archduke and to put an end to the state of anarchy under which the country has so long been labouring'.

But on the whole, peace had returned to this historically tranquil part of Italy; and the incursion of the Banda Garibaldi, whatever the expression on the faces of the inhabitants, and however much Chianti was to be offered to the soldiers, was looked upon with great and understandable alarm.

Hoffstetter was bringing up the rear, with forty horse and twenty foot so that, if there were still offerings of wine, and signs of jollity, that may have been a measure of relief, on seeing the column of 3000-odd pass on. Or is that unfair? It may just be evidence of that talent, more common among Italians than other races, for yielding with grace and style to the inevitable.

This is a prosperous countryside of farmhouses built solidly on tops of small hills: avenues lead up to front gates: hens, turkeys and geese wander around the outsheds and tidy log-piles. We went up and down the small tracks which led between the farms, crossed fords at the bottom of the gentle valleys, enjoyed a quiet walk in which we scarcely saw another human, heard almost no cars. Nor were tractors out at work on Easter Monday; the calm was complete. Only once do I remember our crossing a tarred road, and here there was a party of young men playing that country game in which bowls are delivered, with skilful bias, along stretches of almost straight roads, the aim being that they should roll into the verge as late as possible, if at all.

Sometimes our path led through well-managed young woods, along paths made soft by leaf-mould. In the middle of one glade a pond, leant-over by oak trees, perfect setting for Narcissus, was loud with frogs: as we circled it one after the other, forty or fifty at least, jumped or plopped from the rushes to disturb for a second the still brown mirror of the water.

Each time that we emerged into fields, or stood by the barns of the hilltop farms – admiring the ducks and thinking how good they would be to eat – we looked north-westwards at the chiselled outline of Monte Cetona, with its one high peak; and each time the cross on its summit could be made out a little more clearly.

We paused by a farmyard full of fat guinea-fowl, and a few yards further on, up a white-fenced drive, at last came into view of the distant houses of Cetona, built in tiers up the side of the mountain, with church towers catching the sunlight. Still we were able to walk along rough tracks and footpaths, although the signs of city cares and pleasures were beginning to be evident: parasols set up in one neatly-mown garden, clinks and laughter of a party, coming to us through the neatly-trimmed hedges of yet another restored farmhouse.

'Garibaldi would *never* have attended cocktail parties.'

'He preferred hard cheese.'

Certainly he extolled rigour, and often compared the hardihood of his men on the South American prairies, to the softness of the Italians in their own land. He liked the spare life, scorned luxury. It was believed by one of his followers that a principal reason why he had not chosen to stay and make a fortress of Orvieto – a most defensible city – was that he considered his troops still hadn't suffered enough rain, fatigue, hunger and thirst to fit them for victory. It is not difficult to think of English generals who have made a show of similar abnegation. And indeed, mixed their zeal with a love of ostentation. For all his cultivation of the simple life, Garibaldi knew the value of making an exhibition of himself: his white charger, his black Negro servant (killed in the Defence of Rome), his scarlet poncho. In such careful flamboyance, and setting-apart of himself, it is impossible not to see – whatever its practical justification – the reflection of some need of his nature.

We passed a country house, with dove-grey shutters, and a stream falling down through water-gardens; and took a short-cut towards a vision of Cetona, blessedly nearby. But alas! Reaching a knoll we saw we were still separated from the promised city by a deep and trackless ravine, a jumble of nettles and brambles and rubbish covering the divide.

'What does Christian do in *Pilgrim's Progress*?'

'I'm sure he doesn't go back and take the easy road.'

So we scrambled and bumped down the steep, inhospitable slope, and fought our way once more through nettles and squelchy morass: but did find a crossing, and a path which led between allotments, steeply up towards the walls of this enchanting town, from which, as Hoffstetter says, the eye sees a rich and fruitful countryside, all around.

The streets within the town walls, narrow and steep, occasional cats slinking away round corners at our approach, led us to the central square with its ancient, many-jetted fountain and (more important) to the restaurant Al Rivellino which, after the clock had struck three and while all their other customers were leaving, received with extraordinary warmth and kindness some very tired, dishevelled and dusty walkers indeed. I tried to hide our rucksacks well out of sight. Sheets of vellum parchment pegged to a wall, full of eulogies of previous guests, gave us a moment's – quite unnecessary – alarm about possible prices.

'We must have guinea-fowl after seeing that flock. In fact, I think I can manage two guinea-fowl.'

'Probably cost a bomb.'

'I'm afraid we haven't made nearly as stylish an entry into Cetona as those lancers did.'

'Nor as frightening a one.'

For early on the morning of July 17th, a handful of Garibaldi's soldiers rode into the square, muskets in their right hands, lances in their left hands, reins left dangling on their horses' necks. One story says that the two Tuscan companies which garrisoned the city, learning of their approach when they were already under the walls, had left in such haste and disorder that they had abandoned some of their horses, having no time to saddle them: panic indeed. True or not, the lancers were able to bring back the good news that the town was safe to enter. Garibaldi was resting in a field at the foot of the city, on turf softened by the night's rain, on a morning when the air was as in spring, and the sun shone brilliantly. Brief idyll! He rode up with his army, and soon the square was packed with men, horses, mules, oxen, and the solitary small cannon. Then, for the first and last time, the men were decently quartered. The Chief Magistrate took Anita and Garibaldi under his own roof. Even the horses were stabled under cover, and all the provender found that they needed.

Everyone washed their clothes. Anita was given a dress, quickly run up, of dark green brocade. (This is still to be seen in the museum of San Marino.)

'Cetona seems to have a very good tradition of hospitality.'

'I think I *will* have another one of those excellent guinea-fowl.'

On explaining our pilgrimage – if that is the word – we had been given glasses of champagne on the house. We duly wrote our tribute on the parchment sheets; and I promised myself to examine the records of Garibaldi's splendid reception in the city archives, on the following morning.

The sunny gaiety of the assembly in the square, the cheers and smiles bestowed upon Garibaldi and his men, these visions remembered by old men and recounted to Belluzzi many decades later, are not mirrored in the anguished minutes of the deliberations of the Council, which during those days, stayed in permanent session:

'CONSIDERING that the land of Cetona has been un-expectedly occupied by the troops led by Garibaldi, and that through the lack of forces, and of the time to call them up, any resistance was impossible . . . CONSIDERING that had we wished altogether to refuse the requisitions made, it would have been to expose the land to grave disasters . . . RESOLVED first that the circumstances justify the payment of the Garibaldi contribution . . . second that the Chief Magistrate is authorized to issue as many coupons as are needed to compensate the suppliers of bread and wine . . . (but their expenses cannot be the burden of this community alone) third that the Chief Magistrate is authorized to provide all that is necessary for the provision of his troops and their horses . . . and to honour the coupons issued by the Command of the Troops . . .'

The bill was indeed a heavy one. When it was finally drawn up in October itemized requests had to be met for no fewer than 5500 crowns (say £165,000) from the suppliers of bread, wine, meat, oil, salt, rice, lodging, straw, hay, shoes, trousers . . .

In the immediate crisis there were only 1000 crowns in the civic chest to pay Garibaldi's cash demand and other requests. A whip-round of the richer citizens produced another 1600-odd crowns. Heading the list of the eighteen contributors I saw the name of Terrosi, the nobleman who is remembered in the Murray guide of 1857 as 'liberally allowing his collection of Etruscan antiquities to be visited by travellers': and the same man who provided a banquet in the beautiful rooms which opened on to the long terrace of his palace.

I think he deserves to be remembered. Hoffstetter recalls the evening: '. . . on our return from reconnaissance, the General's lady and the Chief Magistrate came out to meet us, and to lead us on to the belvedere, where the feast was spread out . . . the evening passed agreeably and all too quickly.'

The official records cannot be expected to show sympathy with an invasion which was to cost the community so dear; and it is not unlikely that references to the impossibility of resistance were included with an eye to later justifications. All in all the citizens of Cetona may have been making the best of a bad job, but they were doing it with remarkably good grace. That must be the verdict.

The enchantment of the surroundings of Cetona is well attested by Hoffstetter, in his description of their evening reconnaissance: '. . . this time we took longer on our ride than usual, as our horses were fresh. From the height of the monastery we could see Lake Trasimene, and clearly make out the islands of Maggiore and

Polvese – indeed see the castles and villas of the shore opposite. The mountains and cliff-faces which shut in the lake are those which proved fatal to the legions of Imperial Rome. Close to us, almost at our feet, shone the silvery waters of the small lakes of Chiusi and Montepulciano and, a little further away could be seen the lofty and beautiful Città di Pieve. Sadly we weren't able to enter the ancient city of Clusium, once the capital of the federation of Etrurian cities, and the home of Porsenna. Yet for a long while our gaze rested on it as we thought of ancient times. For us the name of Porsenna had sad associations with the battlefield we had lately abandoned, since Porsenna, like us, had besieged Rome from Monte Verde and the Janiculum . . .'

'Enter Chiusi or Clusium indeed! Hoffstetter was lucky not to have been on *that* particular expedition!'

For it was round about here where one of the most curious incidents of the Retreat took place: indeed the only one upon which Garibaldi himself in his memoirs dwells at all – the taking of a dozen or so monks as hostages. A patrol had been sent out towards Chiusi – and been ambushed. One lancer had been killed, and two taken prisoner, by the Tuscan troops who had erected barricades near the town. Garibaldi wrote in the still-fierce style of his later years: 'Two of our lancers who went forwards as scouts were taken prisoner by peasants belonging to the Bishop of Chiusi. Of a bishop – understand me well: and if I'm not mistaken Chiusi still has a bishop today (in 1872). I asked for my prisoners back, for I certainly believed that they would be in dire peril in the claws of the descendants of Torquemada – and I was denied them. In reprisal I made all the brothers of a monastery march at the head of our column, threatening to have them shot; but the archbishop, a hard man, let it be known that there was plenty of stuff in Italy out of which priests could be made, and didn't want to give me my prisoners back. I believe, besides, that he wanted to see *his* soldiers dead so as to sell them to the crowd as so many sainted martyrs. So I let them go.'

'We must go and see the monastery where they took the fathers hostage.'

'I don't blame him, really.'

First of all, we walked along forest roads at sunset, above the monastery, and gazed at the distant milky waters of Trasimene, as Hoffstetter had done. One spur jutting out into the lake was like a

89

giant's toe. And then we entered, cautiously, by a side gate into a kitchen garden. A lean young man, with an expression of great sadness, was trailing a rake. He appeared not to comprehend our questions, scarcely wished to acknowledge us at all. We pressed further on, into a cloister, unweeded, its paving-stones pushed upwards. A slab of cracked marble rested against one wall. On it we read, carved in sans-serif lettering, the cryptic, one-world creed of MONDO X̱. This was no longer a monastery. No memories of kidnapped monks would be handed down here – so we realized as a smiling sectary approached us, carrying a basket of vegetables which he swung with a vague menace towards my knees.

'Pretend to be a remote descendant of Colonel Forbes. On his mother's side.'

'But we don't know it was he who took the hostages.'

'No matter.'

I hope the Granard family will excuse me. I am sure that not even a renegade Coldstreamer would descend to such subterfuge. Nor indeed was my alias necessary. With great, if rather vague, courtesy we were allowed to see how the restoration of the monastery was proceeding. In the refectory a few Papuan gods looked blankly across the tables. At the end of the room an enormous green Buddha presided. Would the Colonel, I wondered, have liked these latter-day Utopians any better than the Christians they had dispossessed? Probably not. Too ill-disciplined.

'Be careful. He may understand English. These sort of people often do.'

He was smiling silently at us with that look of remote, patient commiseration, not unmixed with underlying menace, which the cult of Eastern religions can sometimes give to their votaries. Here was someone, I felt, who in the most gentle way, and solely for our own good and only after hours of meditation, would not shrink from committing the most outlandish acts. That may be doing him an injustice. Yet oppression did hang in the air, in the stillness of the deconsecrated cloisters. Should I make another attempt to justify our visit: say something which could lead up to an attempt to discover any documents, any memories of any kind about the seizure of the friars? I said, 'Of course, Garibaldi was a great believer in Unity, too. Italy One – Indivisible. Always his creed. You take it one stage further. *World* one and Indivisible . . .'

This was not a success. Perhaps I had not expressed myself very clearly. He shook his head, in sorrow, and padded towards the exit of the cloisters. I noticed he was wearing some Eastern slippers, Burmese possibly. 'I cannot show you any more,' he said, softly. 'It is forbidden.' His face was impassive. I should not have been surprised at all to hear, from the *penetralia*, some boom-boom, gong-beat or drum.

'Why on earth did you suppose Mondo $\underline{X}$ would be interested in Garibaldi?'

'I found the whole thing very spooky. You saw the upside-down crucifix?'

We were walking back to Cetona along a high track. The smell of pine-needles – though faint, because the day had not been hot – was extraordinarily refreshing. Looking down on the city and on the belvedere where Terrosi had so handsomely entertained the General and his staff, I thought how agreeable it was that this wandering band, whatever one might think of their exactions and monk-seizing on one hand, or their heroism and starry patriotism on the other, should have enjoyed their brief interlude in this civilized town, slept between clean sheets, washed their clothes, enjoyed the excellent wine.

At the turn of the century, an ancient eye-witness told his memories to Belluzzi:

'. . . There was the officer Gaggini, an honest, forthcoming intelligent chap who conquered one at first sight. Then Colonel Marocchetti – he had back trouble which made him hobble: always saw him on horseback going to the camp, and on to look-out. And what a splendid and venerable figure Ugo Bassi cut! Cap with a very broad brim, full gathered blouse in black cloth, long grey beard descending to his chest and – what added to his dignity and commanded religious respect – a great black cross which hung from his neck. He rode a most beautiful and spirited sorrel, and he had the firmest seat imaginable, even though the animal was very lively.

'Anita was riding a light bay and rode with great assurance even along our streets poorly paved with travertine, and up our ramped alleyways. A hat of black felt, decorated with a fine feather – black too – covered her mass of hair which fell untidily on to her neck. Was she beautiful? Far from it. Very dark complexion, not very regular features, and smallpox had left its marks. For all that you couldn't look at her except with admiration and ever-growing sympathy.

'Angelo Brunetti [Ciceruacchio the wine-merchant demagogue]
... was simply dressed with a short jacket and hat of thick felt. To all
appearances calm and good-humoured, he could sometimes flare up
if somebody crossed political swords with him. In fact, one day
there was pointed out to him, from the window of the house where
he was staying, an ugly brute of a turncoat priest walking along the
street – a man who'd treated his guests very badly – and
Ciceruacchio took hold of a rifle and pointed it at him and the lady
of the house found it very hard to hold him back.

'Luigi, his elder son, about twenty years old, was a fine figure. He
wore the red shirt, and a beret of red wool with a blue tassel. Blond
hair, cut very short. I often met him, stetson on his shoulder, dagger
in his belt. His good looks, and the knowledge that he was
Ciceruacchio's son, and his solemn air of sadness which made such
a striking contrast with his tender years, made one stop to stare at
him.'

Well might he be solemn. For it was he who had stabbed
Pellegrino Rossi in the neck, to death.

XI

Sarteano
(18-19 July)

THE DEPARTURE OF THE TROOPS from Cetona was by all accounts a jolly occasion. The signal for leaving was given by drums at four o'clock on the afternoon of July 18th. There was a moment of theatre when Garibaldi commanded silence, gazed on the crowds, unsheathed his sword and speaking in a strong, firm voice, promised to 'live for Italy, do all, and will all, for her'. Then he thanked the commune, and left them as a memorial a tricolour pennant.

All this provoked so much enthusiasm that among the cheers several people were heard to call out, 'Long live Garibaldi, King of Italy.'

We took a more modest leave of Cetona – even if the proprietor of the admirable restaurant, who had given us the glasses of champagne, did stop to shake our hands and earnestly wish us well. Perhaps even this may be thought to be a gesture which the short walk to Sarteano – for it is barely six miles away – did not really deserve.

The road commanded distant views eastwards, of the mountains which stand above Lake Trasimene. After half an hour we came to a curve where the road winds down into a deep valley, the hills on our left still precipitous.

'We should identify the Cioncoloni farm.'

'I have every sympathy with that poor Tuscan soldier. He behaved exactly as I should have done.'

We were referring to the incident which Belluzzi thinks may have been the origin of the tale of the Tuscan panic when Garibaldi's lancers first entered Cetona. It was, he says, near the Cioncoloni farm that a Tuscan officer of the small Sarteano garrison suddenly came upon one of the General's patrols. Terrified by the sight, he turned his horse sharply away and scrambled up the steep slope, through woods full of thornbushes and rocky outcrops, so violently that it was a miracle that neither he nor his horse broke their necks. But, in his sudden wheeling-away, his beret had fallen off. This was picked up by the patrol and taken back to Cetona on the top of a pike, which raised a great deal of laughter. However, the trouble for the poor Tuscan was that he now had to appear bare-headed before his fellow-officers. That would have been to cut a very poor figure indeed. However, he solved the problem happily. He deliberately broke his sabre; and invented the tale that he had been in a desperate fight in which both his sabre blade had been shivered, and his beret abandoned.

We took one or two short-cuts, cutting off the zigzags of the steep road which led up again out of the valley. In the rank grass I saw a snake slither – early in the year to see snakes – and my blood ran cold, and I felt sympathy for the Tuscan soldier who was described in a like state of unreasoning panic.

Whether it was through our gesticulations in rehearsing the episode, or through Italian friendliness and pity for two people on foot carrying rucksacks, on our return to the road a Fiat of modest size drew up a few yards ahead of us. This was an unexpected chance to ask whether the farm to which we had been pointing was indeed that of the Cioncoloni. But the driver said:

'No Cioncoloni round here I have ever heard of.' And so I repeated the tale of my mission into his lowered side window. It was a farm-owner of 1849 I was referring to, I explained in conclusion.

'Ah,' he said. 'I am a wine merchant. Get in. I will take you to Sarteano, if you like.'

Had all my explanations misfired? Were we to be taken as ordinary hitch-hikers, after all?

But after a few seconds he tapped on his steering wheel and said, 'My family has a Garibaldi coupon of the time you were talking about. For a horse, I think.'

This must have been one of the coupons which, signed by senior officers such as Forbes, commandeered food, carts and so on. I had been impressed, in the minutes of Cetona deliberations, that the town had immediately decided to honour them. I asked, 'But if you still have it, does that mean that your family are owed a horse by the commune?'

He shrugged his shoulders, simultaneously changed gear. 'As a matter of fact,' he said, 'I have always thought Garibaldi was a great *dormitore* – sleeper.'

This surprised me. It was an aspect of his character I had never considered. Indeed, his tirelessness seemed one of his most amazing qualities. Never to enjoy more than two or three hours' sleep at night on this long trek – and perhaps to snatch an hour or so before the evening march – to sit up telling tales of South American exploits round the camp fire: what kind of sleeper was this? However, I didn't like to contradict somebody who was so kindly giving us a lift.

Or perhaps it might refer to his liking for ladies? I replied, evasively, 'Yes. Well. I imagine after riding from Rome to San Marino, burying his wife, escaping back from Comacchio into Tuscany, he must have wanted a good long sleep.'

He laughed. 'A great sleeper,' he said. 'You must have noticed. You must have seen the plaques in all the towns you have been through – Garibaldi slept here. Why, in Cetona he slept for three days.' He laughed again. Also, he went on, did I not think Garibaldi was a *drogista*?

I should have been less slow-witted. Garibaldi a taker of drugs? My immediate thought was that this might be a part explanation of those amazing, powerful eyes he was said to have had, his soft voice, his patience, his endurance, his long hair even . . . my mind wandered to other eminent drug-takers of the last century, De Quincey, Sherlock Holmes. It would have been opium, of course. This was a facet of his character which I must certainly understand. Perhaps I was still under the influence of Mondo $\overline{X}$?

He stopped his car. We were within sight of the castle of Sarteano which formed such an excellent lookout for the General's staff. '*Drogista*,' he repeated. 'He always took his heroin with him.'

I felt a light tap on my shoulder, from my fellow-traveller.

'You haven't got there yet, have you?'

'Of course. Probably picked the habit up in South America. Surprised none of the authorities mention it, though.'

'Oh, God. Not heroin. Heroine with an "e". Anita. It's a pun.'

'Ah! Anita! *Very* good indeed.'

I hope our driver was satisfied with the reception he got for this awful pun. I have not yet had the courage to try it out myself. I said, after appropriate laughter and thanks, 'I think we had better get out here.'

This was not so much in order to avoid subjection to further jokes – though he might well have several more in stock – as to see Garibaldi's camping ground as described by Terrosi, the noble host of Cetona and collector of Etruscan antiquities. He had followed the General in order to try to persuade him to free the monks – or at least to save their lives.

'All the woody slopes of the hill were covered with tents, most of them under the shade of the green and picturesque copses. Springs of the clearest water rose in the middle of the camp, and surrounded its entire perimeter. On the steepest slope the cavalry were encamped with the carts and the mules, and in the shade of some oaks the captured monks took it in turns to pray and to recite the absolutions of those about to die.'

Well might they be alarmed. Hoffstetter recounts how Garibaldi lectured them. 'You have lighted the sparks of civil war. You call yourself ministers of God, and you are nothing but ministers of the devil etc. etc.' They were to remain as hostages until the two prisoners were released together with their arms and their horses.

However, this is to jump ahead a little to the morning after their arrival. On the previous evening the scene was more peaceful.

Hoffstetter describes how the citizens of Sarteano brought out bread and wine, and hay for the cattle on the hoof. It was easy for the General's young servants to get hold of a great variety of food; and 'the excellent wine helped to make the meal very happy indeed'.

He has a charming account here, of the young servant whose duty it was to look after Anita the heroine. 'Gaetano was very willing and hard-working, only thirteen years old, but with an extraordinarily serious cast of mind. When everyone else was joking and laughing, he hardly opened his mouth. He came from near Bologna, and the General told me that it was usual for boys of that region, at his age, to be serious and determined like this. Gaetano was always ready and present, never turned up late, and his chestnut pony was always the first to be saddled. If he couldn't procure something for his masters, it was quite certain that no one else could. The other boys and stable-lads treated him with great consideration, and did what he wanted them to do. If some officer teased him, he was never embarrassed or out of temper; but those in his good books would sometimes be given a cigar by him – when others had to go without. Often he stuffed one into my pocket, while saying to someone else

96

"Nothing, Sir – nothing I'm afraid." He wore the red shirt, the hat *alla calabrese* with the ostrich feather, and carried a stout dagger in his belt. Alas, some stages before San Marino he fell ill, and had to be left behind.'

The steep, paved streets of Sarteano, up and down which the servants of the General ran procuring delicacies, all too often end in cul-de-sacs, access to the castle which sits on top of the town barred at every other turn. It is like climbing up a maze. In one wall, an old iron hoop, evidently a bell-pull, gave us a moment's hope; but the lady who looked down from the parapet above us, and addressed us, in intervals between the barking of watchdogs, would only say that her masters had left that morning. So, thwarted, we clutched at a few pieces of wild mint that grew out of the crevices of the walls, and wandered back to the Commune where a most courteous Secretary to the Council allowed me a free run of the archives. Here, once more, can be found the familiar plaintive notes. 'Cetona irresistibly overrun . . . prudent in view of the poverty of our forces, to place no obstacle in the way of the Garibaldi column . . . 4500 men armed with a piece of artillery . . . !'

The over-ordering of rations, and the cannon, were serving their purpose.

Yet how does one explain the extraordinary delicacy with which the Austrians, greatly superior in numbers even to the wildest over-estimate of their enemy's force, continued to treat this marauding band, without 'whose dissolution, capture, or at least removal from this continent, Central Italy will not be at peace'?

Those were D'Aspre's words in a letter he wrote from Florence to General Oudinot in Rome on July 13th. Then, he still believed that 'the plan announced by Garibaldi to penetrate into Tuscany is a ruse of war: he is more likely to throw himself into the Abruzzi and try to gain the Adriatic between Spoleto, Norcia and Ascoli'.

A week later, deceived by Garibaldi's counter-marching westwards, he was sending forces southwards from Siena towards the Tyrrhenian coast. Poor intelligence, then, was certainly one cause of the Austrian failure. The rapidity of Garibaldi's night marches, the many feints of the cavalry produced bewildering and contradictory reports from spies. But there are other explanations, too. Belluzzi believes that the Austrians did not relish the prospect of engaging an enemy so irregular as Garibaldi, who was liable to adopt such unorthodox tactics as seizing paddle-steamers. Another possibility we were to see suggested in the archives of Castelfiorentino: the Austrians deliberately wished to let Garibaldi rampage through Italian cities and countryside, in order to 'teach people a lesson', to show them the true nature of the revolutionary brigand.

For his part, at this uncertain stage of the Retreat, encircled though he was by Austrian forces, Garibaldi was finding new courage and heart. Ruggieri says 'At every word that hinted at the wickedness of foreign rule his temper blazed . . . and in the few days in which he was tempted by the idea of reawakening the people of Tuscany to Liberty, you could see in his expression and in his acts a mixture of rage and of joy which then, quickly transformed into disappointment, gave him such a deep frown that no return of hope could remove it.'

'Do you think we should perhaps be a little bolder ourselves?'

'We're becoming idle, you mean?'

Certainly an early morning in which we had advanced a mere six miles, half of it in a humorous wine merchant's Fiat, could not be said to be arduous. So we determined to walk on to the next stage of the Retreat, to Montepulciano, across easy valleys which led to a ridge from which we could see the twin spa towns of Chianciani, skyscraper hotels set in a shell, or basin, of the sulphur-water-bearing hills. Then on, by back-trails, which led steeply upwards through a country rich in well-guarded vineyards, with views over lakes and reservoirs, past domains as grand as those in Burgundy, up and up until we reached sandy paths through young forests, and smelt, somewhere nearby, the smell of charcoal burning, and looked in vain for tell-tale wisps of smoke rising between the trees.

The track on to which we had wandered, in obedience to a compass bearing, led round in a high circle, veering away from the direction of Montepulciano. Garibaldi always liked taking the high way round to any destination, never wanted to be trapped in a plain.

Our problem now was to descend from our height – about 2000 feet – into the right valley. Any hill-walker who knows Italy will appreciate our difficulty. It is only too easy to be tempted by paths which lead into pleasant glades, circle further and further down, finally to descend into a ravine, point in the wrong direction and leave the traveller enthorned and bewildered. Nor are the largest scale maps, those of the Military Geographic Institute of Florence, very reliable guides. Last revised in 1953, they were published before the great era of earth-moving and road-making machines: many paths have been obliterated by these monsters, many new roads built. Even the contours and cliff-faces have suffered at their giant, mechanical hands.

But we were in no hurry to descend, and leave the cool air of the high pinewoods. There was one disappointment. In a clearing we came to what had once been a retreat, or hermitage of Capuchin monks: it was now a restaurant, but boarded up until the summer season came. A forgotten crate of empty wine-bottles set against one wall mocked us.

Yet had we stopped here for lunch, we would have missed the Fattoria Pulcino, the roadhouse outside Montepulciano. How badly that puts it! Its own advertising, on top of the menus, is much more enticing. 'Ancient friary, then farmstead in 1500 . . . restored to its original state by the antiquary Pulcino . . . to offer you, cooked as friars used to cook them, beefsteaks and wine overlooking one of the most beautiful panoramas of the world.'

Even better was to come. In bold type we read 'The essence of the establishment is the grill in the great chimney-place. The wood has been chosen with care and competence so that the embers enhance the natural, genuine savour of the food.' Then an ominous note. 'The prices are determined by the ancient and traditional system of cooking, very refined and costly.' At the bottom of the menu there is a photograph of the head of Silenus, father of Bacchus, looking a little weary.

'We can't say we've not been warned.'

'I particularly like the wood being chosen with *care and competence.*'

'Do you think Anita . . . ?'

This was a reference to Anita's refusal at Montepulciano to join in the banquet prepared for them by the fathers of the monastery in and around which they camped. Such was her aversion to the cloth, that she insisted the food should be brought only as far as the door of her tent where it was taken in by soldiers. A menu which claimed to be cooked in the way that friars cooked, would not have pleased her at all, we thought.

It is fair to add that she was anyway put into a bad mood at Montepulciano, having retired to her tent – pitched in a corner in front of the monastery – in a sulk almost immediately after arrival. A crowd had gathered, curious to see the General and, Hoffstetter says 'as usual the fair sex formed the larger part of it. The General moved among the girls, starting up conversations with the most attractive ones.'

Should we feel, on this subject, as Hoffstetter felt after enjoying *his* delicious meal? Let him speak for himself.

'It's a surprising thing, that everywhere in Tuscany, in small cities like this, one found much more luxury than in the Roman cities which we had passed through in our long journey. However unbelievable it seemed to the tired soldier to enjoy so much friendly show and excellent restaurants, yet such attractions only lasted until our bodily needs were satisfied. I kept on thinking, ever more passionately, of the beautiful Roman country which I had left behind . . . My gaze searched in vain for those tall and noble bodies, that expression of fire, those dark eyes that belong only to the women of Rome.'

'I should not be averse to a romantic encounter in Monte-pulciano.'

'I think we shall have to satisfy ourselves with the sausages, cooked over the embers of wood chosen with care and competence.'

And we did.

XII

Montepulciano

(19–20 July)

A DESERTED CAFÉ, in the central square of Montepulciano, provided shelter, after an afternoon walk which had ended in rain, and a steep climb up a long avenue of cypresses, through whose intervals could be seen, every few yards, the Bramante-like cupola of the church of San Biagio outside the city walls. No one else was about as the rain began to spatter the paved stones. Everything was shut. Any hope of the romantic or improbable was dampened, spirits were lowered.

No one, that is, except a hatless man, in a black plastic mackintosh staring disconsolately at the black rain out of doors. I don't understand the mechanism by which one recognizes the posture, or slouch of an acquaintance when seen from the back; but some instinct made me call out his Christian name loudly, three times. Why should I even have supposed him to be English?

He turned round. Suitable surprise was expressed. Enthusiastic, surprised greetings were exchanged, suitable references made to the General. It was the first time I had recited my speech in English. It had a less impressive ring, to my ears, than the Italian. Perhaps that was because I had grown used to describing myself, with unpardonable exaggeration, as a '*storico inglese*'; but could scarcely claim, to a friend, to be an *English historian*.

However, the reception was gratifying. 'Walked from Rome?' he said. 'You can't possibly have walked from Rome.' He looked distrustfully at our rucksacks.

This echo of the disbelief of the barber who had cut my hair on the eve of our leaving Rome for Zagarolo pleased me. I had forgotten by now how far we had walked. Our pace was leisurely, yes; but as Hoffstetter himself had implied at this stage – and he had three horses – the journey was beginning to be of respectable length. Not without satisfaction I looked at the boots which the shop assistant in Rome had assured me were 'amphibious': and were, indeed, still keeping my feet admirably dry.

'Now we march on to San Marino, over the main Apennines,' I said, rather grandly. The long-distance walker had a right, I felt, to be self-satisfied when confronted by someone who had merely driven down the motorway from Florence.

'I've come here for the wine,' he said. 'You really don't think that's more sensible? The noble wines of Montepulciano? But all the cellars seem to be shut this evening.'

His interest in Garibaldi seemed to be fading. I started to tell him about the tall noble women of Rome, with their dark eyes; but his attention wandered. He said, 'Now I think I could manage to walk to the cellars, if only they were open. That is just about as far as I could walk. So I think you're doing quite well, I really do. But I won't join you, all the same.'

It was appropriate that this encounter should take place in Montepulciano: enthusiastic greetings followed by regretful refusals to join up was just what, on a rather larger scale, the General himself suffered. The Tuscans cheered him on, to such a degree that for a few days he imagined he had some hope of starting a popular uprising, one which would spread quickly to Florence. This, despite the Austrian victory at Novara, despite the restoration of the Grand Duke! It was at Montepulciano that he printed a turgid manifesto:

TUSCANS! Once again Italy is condemned to wallow in filth and infamy . . . . pitilessly downtrodden by those who claim to have been its servants, ever betrayed by those who have betrayed her a hundred times over. This generation had promised to squash him (*sic*) and the promise was false. But we will not lie! We will not bow our necks beneath the yoke of the usurper. Our flag folded in sorrow, riddled with barbarian bullets, has put terror into the Austrians at Luino, into the Bourbons at Palestrina and Velletri, into the French during the campaign of Rome . . . with whatever band of warriors, I shall see that this flag of redemption will wave over our unhappy land . . . we will act as the nucleus for anyone who is ashamed of the dishonour, the abasement, the ruin of Italy . . . OUT foreigners OUT traitors!

This is only an abridgement of an appeal which fell on deaf ears, 'like a burning brand in stagnant water', says Belluzzi.

'Do you think *you* would have responded?'

'The literary style leaves something to be desired.'

In fact, ears were not quite deaf. The authorities of all the towns through which Garibaldi passed announced their adherence to the proclamation of Montepulciano – much good that did him. Ruggieri adds, oddly, 'Let us not blame the noble captain for this resolution, however untimely it may have been: his mind is free from any mean calculations of opportunity.'

Many people might have supposed that calculations of opportunity were exactly what were needed at this stage.

Certainly the Austrians did not scruple to descend to mean calculation. Their deployment of Tuscan troops as the first line of defence meant that Garibaldi was faced with the dilemma either of engaging fellow-Italians in battle, alongside whom he had fought in Lombardy, or of refusing combat. Ruggieri describes his consequent tactics:

'Garibaldi always chose the latter part (that is, refused combat) and emerged with glory. Rapid marches and counter-marches nearly always at night, dividing of the main force into detachments sent in all directions, sudden unexpected concentrations, continual changes – unheard-of tactics with so small a force – were his means. Spreading out his entire forces in line so that they seemed to be three times as many as they were – extraordinary boldness – retreating in haste before larger forces in order to threaten smaller ones, avoiding the uncertain outcome of battle, aiming only to gain ground for freedom of manoeuvre.'

We stood on the steps of the cathedral where we chose to imagine the General had made his proclamation.

'Astride his horse, do you suppose?'

'Could you just try out a few words of his speech? I shall go to the far side of the square and see if they can be heard.'

'But we have absolutely no reason to suppose he *did* make it here.'

'Anyone making a proclamation in Montepulciano must have made it from here. I want you to speak up.'

'I really don't think . . .'

'You can speak in English if you want. But do speak up.'

Some pigeons fluttered up from the paving stones of the square as I attempted a few words, and I seem to remember a road-sweeper looking up incuriously, too. Otherwise my speech produced even less effect than the General's. The experiment was abandoned. A visit to the town hall was rather more fruitful. In its vaulted atrium we found two tributes to Garibaldi; one I believe must have been the earliest we had seen, although it is undated. The tablet of bronze is placed high up on one wall and reads:

> To the honour of the hero of Montevideo
> Giuseppe Garibaldi
> Who having given supreme proof of valour
> In the defence of Italian Liberty
> Here halted on the 19th of July 1849
> The people of Montepulciano
> Dedicated this memorial
> With solemn pomp

The reference to Montevideo would surely not have been made *after* 1860, by which time the renown of his South American exploits would have been overshadowed by his campaign in Sicily and Naples: the story of the *mille*.

The contrast, once again, between the eloquence of the tributes, and the lack of any useful response at the time (even if, as Belluzzi says, the citizens of Montepulciano were drunk with joy to see him) could not but be felt as we stood in the tall, echoing passage.

The room above the restaurant where we stayed was small and dark; and that night, woken often by bells, I could not help thinking that Montepulciano, splendid though its palaces are, and noble though its wines may be, described hyperbolically a century ago as '*d'ogni vino il Re*', nevertheless has a closed air: inbred, turned in upon itself, brooding.

In the morning we walked downhill out of the town, and turned left at a cemetery, enclosed as they often seem to be, in an angle between two roads. Here we climbed a small hillock, and looked back on to black palaces, and pointed towards the monastery – what must once have been the monastery – where Anita sulked, and the General was entertained and fed. Hoffstetter describes the lunch: 'At midday a great table was laid out. The fathers hurried to and fro, full of zeal, to attend to every want of our formidable leader, and saw to it that we were not served by anyone except themselves . . . the monastery had occasion that day to give other proofs of its hospitality, for we learnt later that Forbes and Sacchi with their officers also had a large lunch there, but behind closed doors.'

With a last look we set off in the direction of Torrita, along small lanes, through rolling countryside.

'Just like Devonshire.'

'Surely not. There valleys are far too wide and open. No sunken lanes, either.'

'Just like Devonshire.'

But this was not meant to be taken literally: referring as it did, only to the strange custom of an English officer, during the last war in Italy, to apply this description indiscriminately to any and every terrain provided that it contained at least some hills and streams. In fact, we were walking now through agreeable downland with broad, sinuous folds, tiny rivulets and copses at the bottom of the dips, the fields beside the road of close-cropped turf, from which once we saw two larks rise high in the air. On the skyline to our left the profile of the town of Monte Follonico could be imagined as a two-dimensional stage-set, so clear-etched were its towers and parapets against a solid, but still pale, blue sky.

When we came to the crest of one of those gentle hills, we looked east across a vast landscape out of which rose, fifty miles or so away, the dentellated peaks of the main Apennines, their highest points still swathed in snow.

We could just make out, between the teeth of those far mountains, the curve of a dip which I reckoned must be the pass over which the General was to go a few days later. 'His only thought now,' Hoffstetter says, 'was to reach the main Apennines with his force unharmed, and from there to reach the sea. So he was looking for the most favourable moment to abandon these hills and to recross the Val di Chiana.' Any faint hope of arousing Tuscany was going. It was here, at Torrita, that he turned eastwards again.

Not that he supposed for one second that salvation would be easy. He knew the Austrians were at Perugia, at Siena, with a small garrison at Arezzo, too. Had they any time now marched towards him in any force and engaged him, the catastrophe of San Marino, so Hoffstetter admits, would have taken place much sooner. At

Torrita, they passed an anxious night. Enemy patrols were sighted a few miles distant at Chiusi.

'But the Austrians were so slow: "lazy bohemians" Ruggieri calls them.'

'Does "lazy bohemians" remind you of anyone else . . . ?'

They may have been slow *en masse*, but their scouts were active. Priests were said to have spied for them, and led soldiers along hillcrests. It was of course most important for both sides to choose guides with care and competence, and Belluzzi quotes an old man's memory of having been selected by Garibaldi to lead them on this stage of the journey. Martino Soldati remembered how, as a boy, he had hurried from Torrita to the monastery at Montepulciano, and had hung about at the entrance, hoping for a glimpse of the hero. 'Every time the door opened I looked about the enormous room. I don't know how Garibaldi heard about this Torrita lad who was such a fan of his: the fact is that he had me brought to him and made me sit at table next to him, and said to me several times "I need you as a guide". The meal over, I was ready at the hour of departure, and was mounted, and rode next to the General, who plied me with every kindness and courtesy, and gave me this full cigar case – a green holder with a lady's head painted in colour on it – and I can't tell you how, that unforgettable night, I was transported into a seventh heaven.'

A note of hero-worship creeps into this account, something approaching idolatry, recollected in the sunset of the Risorgimento. Later in his life indeed Garibaldi was often portrayed, blasphemously, in attitudes designed to recall those adopted by nineteenth-century portrayers of Christ: hair falling to the shoulders, eyes gazing straight ahead in resolute tenderness, the hand half-raised in eternal benediction. Perhaps it was round about here that this fashion began; for it was at Foiano that a child was born on the night of his arrival, in the house where the General lodged. Consulted on a suitable choice of name he immediately advised 'ITALIA' and thus the poor baby was christened. Years later, things went further, and he was to be begged to perform the actual ceremony of baptism. (That, however, he declined.)

'We should ask whether there are any ITALIAS alive and well today. The name might well have survived.'

'Better than being called Britannia, anyway. Or America? I believe there are some Americas.'

Montepulciano (*19-20 July*)

We climbed by a side-path, down a steep hill through a white farmstead, turkeys clacking in a yard shaded by old, rambling fig trees: across a narrow valley: then steeply up again, towards the brick-red towers of Torrita – festooned, on the morning we arrived, everywhere with maroon pendants and standards.

But no trace, yet, of any ITALIA.

XIII
Torrita-Foiano
(20-21 July)

OUR WALK IN SPRING SUNSHINE from Montepulciano to Torrita, lark-encouraged, presenting us with wide views of the distant Apennines, had been most agreeable, and not in the least exacting. It left us with time and energy to stroll in the evening to the cypressed cemetery set on a hill just north of the town, from where we could determine the site of Garibaldi's main encampment which, split into three sections, straddled the road leading to Sinalunga – down which it was feared the Austrians might come from Siena.

From here too we looked back on to Torrita, its long row of terraced houses built precipitously on the edge of a deep ha-ha, or empty moat. A casual, untidy line of houses whose windows had shutters of many different colours, somehow giving the air more of a French village – in Burgundy perhaps – than of an Italian town.

As we walked back across the hollow that separated us from Torrita, we came upon an ancient fountain, moss on its stones, watercress growing in the steady trickle of water at its feet. By its side stone pillars rose roofless into the air; in the runnels or troughs of these ruined stables, we were told by a passer-by, it had long ago been possible to water twenty or more horses at once: here, too, the washerwomen of the town would congregate until after the last war.

'Very convenient watering-hole for the General, I daresay.'

'*Water*? For Hoffstetter? You must be joking!'

It was pouring with rain when they left, very early in the morning, still poking and goading the kidnapped monks along at the head of the march. They were not to be let go until after midday, near Foiano. Hoffstetter claims to have interceded for them. The sight of their forced marching was creating a poor impression, he thought, on people who could not know the reasons why they had been taken prisoner in the first place – especially as they all walked with hands clasped together in continuous prayer, and wore the most holy of expressions on their faces.

Their release, however, by no means spelt the end of the persecution of monks. It was, for example, reported in the *Statuto* of Florence that at Torrita the commander of the rearguard, not content with imposing a levy of 100 crowns on the municipality, also seized the vicar, and freed him only after a ransom of another 100 crowns had been paid – by the Church, presumably.

'Relatively modest kidnappers, you must agree, by modern standards.'

'Don't you think Anita would have been amazed that anyone should pay *any* ransom for a monk?'

We were throwing olive-stones into the canal – the *canale maestro* – of the Chiana, by whose straight, deep-sunken paths, almost as wide as towpaths, we picnicked at leisure on our walk from Torrita, via Foiano, towards our next stop at Castiglion Fiorentino. I rather think that we spent little time on talking about the poor monks, and much more time on whether, at certain seasons of the year, it might be possible to canoe all the way from Pisa up the Arno, along the canal, and down the Tiber to Rome. A few elder branches trailed into the shallow waters of the opposite bank, lightly rippled by a breeze. To the north and south we could see, in a line so long and so straight that the last examples visible were tiny toys in perspective, a succession of iron bridges carrying roads and tracks: the one nearest to us, to judge from its curlicues and flourishes, a century or more old.

On both occasions that Garibaldi and his force made their uncertain way over this canal, with its treacherous, supporting criss-crosses of reedy ditches, they were drenched with rain: horses stumbled in the pitch dark, and the fear of being attacked by the Austrians before they could reach the far side of the plain and the relative security of the mountains, pressed upon them. In fact, Austrian accounts make it clear that Paumgartten's chief concern was to protect the city of Cortona from the bandit's unwelcome attentions, rather than to pursue him. That, of course, Garibaldi was not to know, although later in his life, might he perhaps have been sourly amused to learn that his efforts to magnify his force had been so successful – in reputation if not in fact? I wonder.

'But one mustn't suppose that Garibaldi was altogether without a sense of humour.'

'Such as?'

'Well, he called one of his donkeys PIO NONO.'

'As the barber of Monterotondo told you.'

Traversing this country ourselves, unstumbling in the breezy afternoon, we made out the city which the Austrians protected as a white splash, set up high on the black wall of mountain-face which, to all appearances, rose sheer from the dead level of the green, fertile, watery plain.

It was as though two different surfaces met each other: like a cliff rising steep-to, seen across an expanse of still water. To enhance the illusion of being at sea there came from a nearby hut a persistent throb, as of a ship's engine. Barns and huts of all sizes dot and dash this flat terrain, storing crops, tools, agricultural machinery of all kinds; but this pulsing noise didn't sound like a tractor. A ditch separated us from its source. Wishing to exchange a few words with the guardian of the engine, we scrambled across, and peered into the black entrance of the cabin. Here a great pump was sucking water from the marshy ground, dredging it up to disgorge into the ditch on the other side. It had been left unguarded, save for a brindled dog, chained to a pipe, which wagged its tail and slunk into a corner. Decipherable on a brass plaque on the engine's side was the name of an English firm in Grantham, and the date of 1923. The planks of the deck shook as it pumped. An occasional backfire, like gunshot, made me start.

Somewhere not far beyond where we stood, an Austrian patrol was met and put to flight. More dramatically, an Austrian soldier, disguised as a peasant, was captured by the same troop of cavalry under Major Migliazzi, and was found to be carrying a despatch from the officer commanding at Perugia, promising to send reinforcements urgently requested by the small garrison at Arezzo. Taken to Garibaldi and questioned, he revealed that four companies were about to arrive from Cortona at any moment. On this news, the General withdrew all the patrols in the area, and concentrated them for an ambush. One hundred paces to the north of the bridge over a small stream near Montecchio – towards which we were now walking – he stationed one company of his best troops, in line, facing the road, using a ditch as cover. A second company, also in line, was stationed two hundred paces down the road, hidden by a high hedge. Finally three companies with a detachment of cavalry, were placed a further two hundred paces down, using a few houses as cover and disposed in column ahead, ready to attack the Austrian van. One officer remained up at the bridge to give notice of the enemy's arrival. The first company was to allow the enemy to proceed; and take possession of the bridge, and cut off the enemy's retreat, once the second company had discharged its second round of fire, which in turn was ordered to point its rifles through the hedges and start firing only after the head of the enemy column had already passed. This discharge was, indeed, the signal for springing the ambush.

The gap between the tall hedge and the houses was carefully left open and unencumbered, since it was thought likely that the enemy would knock up the occupants and ask for information. These, however, were packed off to Castiglion Fiorentino, and some of Garibaldi's men were disguised and put in their place. Several patrols rode up and down the stream – which is easily forded – and a few went as far as the canal. The General left the scene only when he was absolutely satisfied that everyone understood his orders.

And after all the preparation the Austrians decided after all not to advance beyond Cortona!

I describe this abortive ambush in such detail, following Hoffstetter, because it seems evidence of such an extraordinary level of discipline, morale and tactical resourcefulness on the part of an army which had been more or less continuously on the march for three weeks, had no headquarters to sustain it, could not hope for any reinforcements, knew that it was surrounded by an enemy greatly superior in numbers – and had just endured an extremely disagreeable and dark night of downpour.

There is an epilogue to this tale. The Austrian despatch-bearer who had been captured in disguise as he tried to catch the post-chaise for Arezzo, was found to come from the Trentino – a region which, even though it was largely German-speaking, was in Garibaldi's eyes part of Italy One and Indivisible. Since the man was not in uniform he might well have been summarily shot, and must have feared for his life. Hoffstetter describes the subsequent scene,

'Being Italian by birth the General wished to do him no harm. Instead he contented himself by ordering the man to be put back into uniform (which was found in the post house), and parading him before the army. "What a sad thing it is," he said to his men, "that our oppressors should find *Italians* to fight against our people! See how suited this strange hat, and this grey jacket is to an *Italian*! I hereby grant him his life, because he is not worth the bullet that would be needed to kill him." The soldiers replied with VIVAS to Garibaldi and to Italy, cursing its oppressors.'

For us, it was evening. We climbed up, through olive groves, to the ruined castle which crowns the hill above Montecchio, and looked back west across the Val di Chiana, to the hut with the aged pump, the lines of irrigation canals, the road and the site of the failed ambush immediately beneath us; and spared a thought for the unfortunate man who had so vainly tried to hide his Austrian uniform in a post office.

'Worse than being in disgrace at school.'

'And so much is lost in post offices nowadays. *Very* bad luck that it turned up.'

Eastwards the view was towards mountains, and deep valleys leading up towards the high ridges that separate the tributaries of the Arno from those of the Tiber: everything turning black beneath swishing clouds, some of which separated, as we looked, to reveal a peak, and the faint outline of a cross on its summit. For a few minutes we circled the outer walls of the castle, treading gingerly over planks laid across trenches which advertised works of restoration, climbing up and down terraces of olive trees, past two tethered goats, and came to the barred, front gate. The iron hoop of a bell failed to work, the speech I had prepared to gain admission was never uttered, and we took the stony track downhill.

It was not disagreeable, as we started to walk along the straight road past the café (which I think was on the site of the *osteria* which Hoffstetter says was near the ambush-stream), to hear the screech of the tyres of a red Alfa Romeo, savagely braked. We were being offered a lift, and for the second time since leaving Rome we accepted. This time however it was no wine merchant with a repertoire of puns, but a dedicated motorist who drove silently, furiously, leather gloves poised, without strain, on the steering wheel. The fury of his driving – his cornering, his changing gear – and the continual hiss which may have come from his mouth or from his car (I could not tell which), precluded attempts at conversation, so that for the second time that day I was unable to produce my well-rehearsed Garibaldian references.

Once he spoke, though. Coming to a crossroads he said, jerking his head sharply, 'The road to La Nave.' 'Why La Nave? I mean why *called* La Nave?' I was curious to know. Ship seemed a strange name for a village. Once more I was reminded of my sensation, when walking across the plain, of having been at sea. But he shrugged his shoulders, and accelerated.

At the southern entrance to Castiglion Fiorentino he braked again, with even more violence, and opened the door to let us out, scarcely waiting to listen to our thanks. Perhaps we had grown used to a gentler progression. We climbed up the steep, narrow streets, enquiring after *pensiones*, until we reached the central square. Here the municipality is housed in a noble seventeenth-century palace: on the side opposite, the arches of a long colonnade give views of the mountains – views of great variety, for through each arch you enjoy different compositions of red-tiled roofscapes and green hillsides.

Murray in 1857 recommended the Leone Bianco, 'a very fair village inn, with a civil landlord'. The White Lion is no longer to be found, but underneath a small porch, by the Arezzo gate, there is a very fair *pensione*, with a civil landlady. Indeed the rooms were so agreeable and the bathrooms offered such hot water and such splendid views too, that we proposed to spend two nights, and devote one day to the archives, should these seem promising.

❦ XIV ❧
Castiglion Fiorentino
(21-22 July)

I T IS TIME ONCE AGAIN to present the other side of the case, and
to show events as they appeared to those who had to endure what
was, in their experience, a thoroughly disagreeable army of occupation.

There exists, in the archives of Castiglion Fiorentino, a
manuscript written in an old man's wobbly hand, in 1876 on the
occasion of the unveiling of the statue to Garibaldi: the one which
still stands in the piazza that bears his name. The writer declared his
position frankly. Indeed, he says that the best moment of the
ceremony was when someone – a foreigner – broke into praises of
the capture of Rome by the French (but was at once shut up like a
buffoon). Here is my abridgement of his tale of those tumultuous
days of Garibaldi's passage. I am sorry to say it contains a brief
account of some pretty rough behaviour by Citizen Colonel Forbes.

'Impossible to think of any city which ought *less* to celebrate the
passage of Garibaldi than Castiglion Fiorentino . . . we will do well
to remember just what did happen twenty-seven years ago.

'The French and the Austrians, disdaining to come to grips with
Garibaldi, contented themselves with following slowly on his heels,
and letting the people have a taste of the consequences of their
fanaticism for him.

'Perhaps Castiglion Fiorentino would have been spared had
pretext not been given . . . There was a new chemist at Agnolesi's, a
Florentine called Giovanni Nannini; three or four days before
Garibaldi's coming he was heard to say, publicly, in the café of
Caetano Zoi, what a very close resemblance his hero bore to Jesus of
Nazareth – and how before long he *would* be the Jesus of Nazareth
of Tuscany. Of course the government of the Grand Duke had been
restored, so the chemist was clapped into gaol at once.

'That displeased the friends of his party, so much so that when
Garibaldi, who was at Foiano on the morning of the 21st, heard of

it, he thought he might as well take advantage of the feelings that had been aroused; so, in the belief that the town might rise in revolt, he proceeded to Castiglion Fiorentino by the La Nave road, instead of going the direct way to Arezzo. Thus he delayed by a day his arrival in that city, where there really was some hope of an insurrection – but which in the event shut its gates in his face. When Garibaldi arrived in Castiglion Fiorentino, he had the five or six policemen who were there disarmed, and let the chemist out of prison; and the magistrate Moyelli, who was old and rather timid, even apologized to him.

'The chemist duly went to Garibaldi's tent next morning to offer him his thanks, and was invited to follow him. He declined, on grounds of age . . . Soon after Garibaldi left, the police returned, arrested him and took him to Florence where he paid the penalty for his conduct, and from there he wrote that he would never forget Castiglione! (*No wonder!*)

'Although a very few liberals had got it into their heads that Garibaldi was sure to come because of the chemist's imprisonment – or at least hoped so, and made a noise about it – it is safe to say that the town as a whole did not expect him, and his sudden arrival terrified everybody. Prudence seemed the wisest course.

'Some monks got away to their country retreat . . . the Capuchins stayed indoors that day and took in the things which people brought to them for safekeeping, the novices were terrified and set to prayer, the Piarists took things more calmly, the ordinary priests mostly hid at home. None of their fears should seem excessive, since it was known from the report printed in the Tuscan Monitor that fourteen friars of Cetona and the subprefect of Montepulciano had been taken hostage, and released near here at Foiano . . .

'The Chief Magistrate Reatelli, urgently summoned from Castiglion del Lago, returned to the city in the evening . . . meanwhile the Canonico Tommasi, in his capacity as Prior had taken it on himself to provide hay and other needs for the animals which Garibaldi had with him which included oxen for slaughtering. He was most prompt in furnishing all that every Garibaldino asked for, believing that in that way the worst would be avoided.

'But on the following morning – Sunday – Garibaldi levied a contribution of 1000 crowns on the town. As the Commune did not have enough money to pay it on the spot, private citizens were asked for immediate help. Among those to whom it turned was P. Serafino, administrator of the monastery of St Francis, who was asked for 100 crowns. He brought it, unwillingly, to the Commune after ten o'clock. Seeing him come, the Chief Magistrate went out to meet him – and thanked him, saying that the sum had in fact already been found. The Commissariat Forbes who had seen the Brother and had heard what had been said broke into a tirade against the Chief Magistrate: "The Brother brings money and you, you thief, do you refuse it? No, no, Brother, now you've got two hours to fetch me five hundred crowns – or else be made hostage."

'P. Serafino was struck dumb with terror, and the Chief Magistrate was afraid that he would be taken hostage too . . . But who had told Forbes that the convent was in a position to pay 500 crowns? "*You've got it,*" he said. Well, the Prior was not at all well-disposed towards the Brothers and it was thought that he might have hinted to Forbes that the monastery was able to pay, perhaps hoping that the higher the monastery's contribution, the lower would be the town's. The monastery was in fact able to contribute 500 crowns, because it had been paid to them a few days earlier by the Commune in compensation for some ground expropriated to make the road to Palazzo del Pero.'

(To comment in passing, this explanation has a familiar Italian ring to it. Road contracts seem to bring out the worst in people. And how common, how regrettable the use of public misfortune to pay off private scores!)

But to continue: 'P. Serafino, recovering his courage, realized that the Field Adjutant Marocchetti was a more humane man than his brother officer Forbes; so he approached him, and begged for a reduction. Marocchetti decided to take Serafino to Garibaldi . . . going out of the Commune with him, and walking through the streets, the people were afraid that he was being taken hostage and thronged after him. Marocchetti entered the General's tent, the General was there, Serafino went into the tent, and the General reduced the levy to 200 crowns. Serafino at once brought that to the Commune but Marocchetti refused to take it, saying that he wanted to pay a visit to the monastery after lunch. It was during this visit that Serafino jokingly made him a present of a bottle of Vino Santo – which led to a further reduction of 50 crowns.

'The Chief Magistrate also went to Garibaldi's tent and obtained a reduction from 1000 to 565 crowns; but the Garibaldini roamed the town, invaded shops – several of which stayed open despite regulations to the contrary – and took clothes, leaving coupons in exchange which the Commune had to redeem. And the prices the shops charged were very high.'

A long catalogue of the misdeeds of the Garibaldini follows and includes the theft of a precious sixteenth-century map of Tuscany, which was eventually retrieved – at a price – and is today back in the municipal library.

The writer observed how very badly equipped and turned-out most of the soldiers were, with the exception of a few officers who still wore smart uniforms and had valuables with them. He remembered, too, men who showed signs of wanting to desert: a few were seen crying, many entered the churches and attended mass. Ugo Bassi, dressed as an officer, went to confession, first laying down his arms.

They all left on Sunday evening, shortly after rumours ran through the city that the Austrians were coming. These proved true, and soon about 1000 troops entered the city, very warily.

There follow, in this account, several pages which describe the politics which surrounded the erection of the statue in 1876. The final paragraph bears quoting:

'One mustn't trust the extravagances of the newspapers and of the Liberals which would have us believe that the citizens were delighted to raise a monument to Garibaldi. A few ignorant fanatics have considered that they acted in the name of everyone; but the majority, and those of good sense, see in the affair, one of the usual demonstrations of the tyrannical party in power . . . and let us remember that while the inscription was being composed for the statue, another and more truthful "inscription" was going the rounds. This one was spontaneous, natural, on everyone's lips – and Garibaldi himself wouldn't be able to complain of it for it is no less than the truth:

> GIUSEPPE GARIBALDI
> Qui venne, e si attendò;
> mangiò, prese quattrini, e se ne andò.

> OR   Here
>   Giuseppe Garibaldi
>   came, stayed, ate,
>   took money and left.'

The librarian recited to me this disrespectful triplet as, with great kindness, he escorted me to his library and opened it, out of hours. Among the many treasures I was shown was a first edition of Diderot's great encyclopaedia and, if this is not strictly relevant to my tale, one could at least plead that the arrival in Italy of the ideas of the Enlightenment during the last years of the eighteenth century, gave birth to the political aspirations which the Congress of Vienna in 1815 froze but could not destroy, and which after so many trials, conspiracies, defeats and revolutions ultimately led to the freeing of Italy from the rule of Austria and of popes and princes.

But why should the English continue to fuss over Garibaldi? This was a puzzle to the librarian. Consider his vanity, arrogance, political naïvety, fanaticism – his sheer tiresomeness. Might it be due, I attempted unsuccessfully to answer, to a certain type of English upbringing? Simple-minded heroes, selfless men of action, fascinate schoolboys. But my halting apologia wasn't really necessary; for it turned out that Castiglion Fiorentino possesses several relics of the General of which they are modestly proud. On the wall behind the Mayor's desk there still hangs the tricolour, sewn by ladies of the city in aid of the Garibaldi 1859 million-rifle fund. And the swords and uniform of an officer of the Sicilian Expedition, a native of the town, is preserved in the museum. Given his hat, I turned it over and read on the inside of the crown CHRISTY'S BEST; and was glad to see that a London hatter's work was still in excellent shape: Captain Bolsi's head was smaller than mine, or else I should have asked to try it on.

Light showers, slanting across the piazza outside the Commune, and sudden gusts of wind, would have made one of Christy's best hats very welcome. Our walking plans, after a day of leisure, were still indeterminate. On the one hand, the General himself had made a long reconnaissance on the morning of the 21st, up the deep valley that leads to Castellonchio. Some of his patrols were seen in Pieve di Chio. This would have made a splendid walk. On the other hand, the General in the end – 'just like him, he always tricked everyone', says Hoffstetter – decided to take the main road straight to Arezzo. A bold move, for the Austrians might easily have closed in on him along this way. But all the evidence suggests that, perhaps as early as Montepulciano, he had had reports of incipient uprisings in Arezzo. There was talk of his being able to get hold of 2–300 carbines there, of the youth of the town digging up buried arms, of the small garrison of Austrians preparing to leave. His hopes of resurrection, and of recruitment, were dying hard.

Should we go by the adventurous and picturesque mountain paths? We climbed in the evening a short distance up white gravel roads, from which tracks led off at each curve into terraces of olive trees, and looked down on the small plateau where the General and Anita and the staff had pitched their tents. Above us was the dark interior of the hills, a few tiny white farms and chapels lit by occasional shafts of sun. The weather was pretty threatening.

'It looks very wild and steep. And anyway that's not the way the General did take.'

'You are simply looking for excuses to take the easy way. Typical.'

In hindsight, I regret having chosen the low road to Arezzo, instead of the mule-tracks and paths over the mountains. None of these climbed to more than 2000 feet and had the clouds cleared there would have been splendid views towards the horseshoe valley of the Casentino, and the winding Arno. To compensate for our indolence, to clutch back some notional virtue, we inflicted upon ourselves a dawn start the next morning, leaving the comforts of our *pensione*, and the civilized delights of Castiglion Fiorentino – a laundry had cleaned all our clothes – shortly after six o'clock. The air was fragrant with the smell of every kind of pine tree since for half an hour or so the road is bordered, on both sides, by a vast nursery garden. This seemed to be used as a sanctuary for birds too, for an ascending dawn chorus surrounded us; and once, at the far end of a long avenue, I caught sight of a many-coloured fan, and heard a screech, which surely must have been a peacock's. Then, to the left of the road, also down a long avenue, a hoot announced the slow passage of an immensely long train of goods-wagons; here we were within two or three kilometres of the main Florence–Rome line.

Sometimes, leaving the road, we walked through fields, and crossed planks laid over the many small streams which rush down from the mountains into the Val di Chiana; then, coming to the low wall of a vineyard, retired again to the long stretches of highroad which lead slowly upwards in a series of low undulations. Villages came and went; and, although the Italians are early risers, at the beginning of our walk the clank of the shutters of newspaper kiosks, opening up, was the only sign of activity – that, and a solitary girl outside a café sweeping the pavement. To reach the low pass at the village of L'Olmo, where the road briefly seems to be cut through rock, we took about two and a half hours – resisting, once or twice, the temptation to join groups of old men and women waiting for a bus. From L'Olmo the valley opens out to give wide views of the prosperous city of Arezzo, with its outlying villas and occasional parklands, its broad peripheral roads, and clusters of light industry. This was the largest town we had seen, let alone entered, since leaving Terni, and I felt for a moment our shabbiness, our boldness in daring to re-enter busy civilization on foot.

Here Hoffstetter was assailed by other, nobler thoughts. For the rearguard remained for a while at L'Olmo, to give advance warning of any possible approach of the Austrians coming from Perugia. As in the ruins above San Gemini, where he dreamt of toga'd Romans standing under the great, isolated arches, so here he found time to reflect: 'In this position before Arezzo, the ancient Aretinum, probably on the heights above this pass, Flaminius lay in wait for the Carthaginian army: in vain, for Hannibal passed in front of his position, turned, and marched down the Chiana, *via* Chiusi towards Perugia, finally to draw up his men before the Consul, on the shores of Lake Trasimene.'

A little further on, about 100 yards before the gates of the city, the officers gathered to hear the report of Major Migliazzi who had ridden all the way round the walls with a troop of cavalry. Everyone agreed that it would be practicable to invade the city with the aid of a couple of ladders. A few shots of the cannon would be enough to open the gates. But the General took no decision . . .

Meanwhile a prisoner was taken, a postilion bringing a despatch from Stadion at Siena to Paumgartten at Perugia. Hoffstetter describes the scene in the hut near here, where he was taken. '. . . a single candle, near the General, burned on a block of wood, the only piece of furniture, and threw a dim light on the group. I was on my knees before the candle, translating the despatch, which was written in German. All around in the half-dark, could be seen the bronzed and bearded faces of the staff; and in one corner, half-dead with fright and guarded by two lancers, lay the poor postilion . . . before leaving the wretched hut, the General had the postilion brought up to him. In mortal fear the man fell at his feet, begged for his life, and swore that he would never, ever again perform any such service for the Austrians. Instead of punishing him, the General simply advised him not to be caught a second time.'

The intelligence that the despatch contained was valuable: it revealed the strength of the enemy's forces – about four battalions each at Siena and at Perugia. Stadion complained of the civil unrest which hindered his movements, but hoped to join forces with Paumgartten. It was thought that Garibaldi was trying to make for Venice, and his numbers were put at 4000 men, with several cannon.

As Hoffstetter says, the despatch reveals the poorness of the enemy's intelligence, and the lack of his will. If only the Austrians had pressed hard on his heels, they would quickly have realized that Garibaldi had little more than half the force which they thought and only one old, faulty piece of artillery.

We had dawdled, on a morning which grew warm as the sun rose, on the outskirts of the city idly attempting to find a plausible location for the 'wretched hut' a hundred yards from the gate. Now a depository of calor gas cylinders? A petrol station? A shop selling typewriters? Or indeed the café into which we went for a fairly well-earned breakfast?

'I suppose, strictly speaking, we shouldn't go into the town at all. We should be rejected, turned away.'

'*You* can be an outcast if you want to. You look quite like one.'

'There might be something up there. About half a mile away uphill. Santa Maria. Though on my map there's only a church there. That's where Garibaldi . . .'

'Nobody is going to stop me getting my breakfast *now*.'

The chapter of the closing of the gates of Arezzo was about to begin. Garibaldi himself had been one of the first to approach the gates, and had been startled to find his way barred by a mixed patrol of Austrian and Italian soldiers. Hoffstetter was disappointed at the delay in attempting to force entry: he writes, 'We had arrived within cannon-shot at about eleven o'clock in the evening . . . a little after midnight I threw myself on the ground amongst my horses, rather fed up that we had not attacked Arezzo yet, but hoping that the assault would take place tomorrow.'

Antonio Guadagnoli, Chief Magistrate and minor poet, had been responsible for closing the gates, and it is to him that I will now briefly turn.

Arezzo

(22-23 July)

THREE YEARS AFTER he had by his own lights, saved Arezzo from Garibaldi and possible civil war, Antonio Guadagnoli visited London for the Crystal Palace Exhibition, and put his first impressions into verse –

> Eccomi in Londra! Oh Dio, che musi seri
> nessun sorride ed ogni labbro e muto
> Guardan con noncuranza gli stranieri
> e nessum li degna d'un saluto
> Sconta di noi che siam assuefatti
> a cavarci il cappello perfino ai gatti!

which I roughly translate as –

> Here I am in London! Lord –
> Native faces, how they're bored!
> Lips drawn tight, no smiles, nought said,
> Strangers from abroad cut dead.
> How unlike us, raising hats
> Even, as we pass, to cats!

In keeping with his gift of light verse, Antonio Guadagnoli possessed an engaging irreverence. When at last, at very long last, his rich uncle and promised benefactor died ('I know about the Eternal Father but the eternal uncle is a bit too much,' he had once complained), he answered a friend's enquiry with a suitable sigh, saying, 'My uncle and I have passed to a better life.' An agreeable man, fond of his food, a most dutiful citizen and leader of the Moderate party, who will blame him now for his actions in July 1849? Yet it really will not do to try to excuse him, as his biographer

has done, on the grounds that he was acting under higher orders
from the prefect. The archives at Arezzo show that the resolutions
of the council under his chairmanship were unanimous. A long
minute written on July 27th and signed by him, shows how the days
of threatened invasion were seen from within the city walls.

'The gentlemen assembled, KNOWING the critical circumstances
in which our city was placed, threatened with attack by the
Garibaldi band encamped on the hill of Santa Maria . . . KNOWING
how the Royal Troops . . . and the few gallant Austrian troops,
although convalescent . . . and a band of worthy citizens especially
enrolled – laboured night and day to keep internal order . . .
HEREBY RESOLVED unanimously that the Chief Magistrate be
charged to lay before His Excellency the Minister of War the
exemplary conduct of the above-mentioned troops, imploring him
to make known to them the thanks which the Municipality of
Arezzo renders to them . . . (and resolve) that this deliberation be
transcribed into the protocol as a memorial to posterity of these
events.'

This is a considerable abridgement. But the emphasis on the
keeping of internal order in this vote of thanks confirms both the
dangers of civil insurrection and the wisdom of denying entrance to
Garibaldi's troops. Hard although it may be to believe nowadays,
Arezzo has a history of violent disturbance; in 1799 the citizens rose
against the French and terrible atrocities were committed; in 1847
the bread riots were especially ugly.

Another account in the Protocol describes how with the
authority of the local government, and the subsequent approval of
Count Stadion, the commune met Garibaldi's requests by sending
him considerable quantities of provisions in the hope that this
would prevent the very much greater losses that might otherwise be
suffered by the 'poor people of the countryside'.

Throughout the minutes the savage band of Garibaldi stands out
in contrast to the behaviour of 'the most illustrious Austrian
troops'.

In fairness, Tuscan cities, unlike those in Lombardy and the
Papal States (Milan and Bologna for example) had had no
experience of the brutality of which the Austrian army was capable.
Even although it may have been most mistaken of the Grand Duke
to have allowed himself to be restored with Austrian aid – the
municipality of Florence was spontaneously negotiating for his

return early in 1849 – the army had not fought in Tuscany, save to quell a brief resistance in Leghorn. On the other hand, the citizens of Arezzo had very good reasons to fear their own mob uprising. The prudence of the council was, I think, commendable.

Their motives for bringing out to the encampment excellent supplies of wine and food, which included meat, salami, rice and some remarkably *white* bread, were correctly guessed by Garibaldi. They wished to remove any pretext for attack. Nevertheless, his men were very disappointed indeed that no such attack was mounted. They had, as at Orvieto, been engaged in all the preparations: ladders were constructed for scaling the walls, the solitary cannon was pulled into position and pointed at the gates. Weary and dispirited by continual forced marches, continual pitching and breaking of camp, July sun and July deluges, they were elated at the prospect of battle, in which at last their fortunes would be put to the test. That this was declined when it became known that the city was defended by a handful of Austrians, convalescent Austrians at that, made them wretched; and Hoffstetter suggests that from this moment decline in morale became very steep. Yet in retrospect he considered that Garibaldi was right. At the time he had asked the General why he delayed, and received the reply *verbatim*: 'I think as you do, but what would we do with the wounded? We can't take them with us, and if we left them here, they would be shot by the Austrians. Arezzo is important to us only for morale – we couldn't dream of stopping here – we should be surrounded in next to no time.'

Not that this was the reason which Garibaldi gave for his forbearance to the deputation from the council. To them he said that his respect for the citizenry was the sole reason for his not resorting to force.

Yet the overriding motive was almost certainly neither the one he gave to Hoffstetter, nor the one he gave to the deputies. His objective was to reach Venice, with as many men in as good a condition as possible. So were his different replies due to confusion, or to deviousness? Why had he made this diversion to Arezzo, if he now refused to lift more than a finger? What indeed did he hope to achieve in Venice – which fell to the Austrians within a few weeks, as it surely must have fallen, even with the advent of his tired army?

I suspect that all these motives and doubts were mixed up in his honest mind. If so, it says a lot for his leadership that confusion was not apparent to those who followed him.

'Not everyone who is confused shows it as much as, well . . .'

'*Me?* Anyway, I don't pretend to be a leader of men.'

'I suppose you think you're good-natured, moderate. Garibaldi would definitely not have approved of you *at all*.'

'Too bad.'

'So you told me. He hated lukewarm people – wets.'

I remember our briefly discussing the Arezzo imbroglio while we waited for a free chess-table in the civilized café opposite the Church of San Francesco – the only one I know in Italy in which chess-tables outnumber fruit-machines. Once past the throng at the main counter you come into a large room, high-ceilinged, dark-walled, whose old-fashioned lamp fittings and potted plants give it something of the air of an Edwardian tearoom. Here there congregated, or at least did so on the evening of our visit, the bourgeoisie of Arezzo – doctors, lawyers, pensioners, the descendants of Antonio Guadagnoli: wearing brown suits and hats, their pommelled walking-sticks placed carefully by the chairs. The game itself was played with far more passion and pace than in England; at each move one of the tall wooden pieces was banged down furiously on the board, another hand banging with equal fury on the top of the clock. Exclamations of disgust and incredulity were opposed by the serene expression of anticipated victory. No bored faces, closed lips, silence here.

We had come to the café, our necks stiff from gazing upwards at the frescoes of Piero della Francesca in the church across the way, which unravel the dream of the Emperor Constantine, the battle of Aleppo, and the discovery of the True Cross: at the coiffed ladies who stand in adoration, with faces of the utmost calm, still and impassible: at the priests with tall hats like bakers: at the warhorses, broad-chested, caparisoned, rearing, snorting; at the soldiers with their pikes one of whom, at the top left-hand corner of one wall, appears to have just been dismembered, his head now lying between his feet.

Of all the incidents of Garibaldi's Retreat and even granted that Arezzo naturally suggests itself because of the presence of these frescoes, the scene which is most worthy of a painting on this scale would be the arrival of the General and the bearded friar Ugo Bassi, close beneath the city walls, and their encounter with the deputation who had come out to meet them, while from the battlements above a few white-coated Austrian soldiers (some of them perhaps bandaged if they were convalescent?) look down in silent, wary apprehension, not moving. There is, in this scene as described by Belluzzi, something of the sense of being in the still centre of dramatic events, the momentary timelessness (if the oxymoron be allowed) of which Piero della Francesca is the master.

Attempting to walk round the perimeters of the old city of Arezzo, in the hope of identifying the possible ways by which Garibaldi's army beat its retreat during the dark night of July 23rd, was a thankless task. Battlements have been bulldozed, landmarks obliterated by broad avenues, vast furniture stores, tenement blocks, one of our consolations being that parts of the army, too, got utterly lost that night.

The city was enlivened on the day of our visit, and made even more crowded and bustling than usual, by the holding for charity of a children's market, scattered over a wide area and blocking street after street, in which all the stalls, selling second-hand clothes and comics and toys and household odds and ends, were run with admirable flair by boys and girls, nearly all of whom appeared to be under twelve. They parodied their elders, mimicking acts of bargaining and echoing familiar marketing catch-phrases. 'I must be mad, I'm *giving* it away,' I heard one tiny child shout, holding a small broken plastic soldier (not, alas, Garibaldi) as high up in the air as he could.

This diversion, too, consoled us for our failure.

Hoffstetter's tale of his confusion, as he floundered in pitch darkness in the environs of Arezzo, reminds me a little of the bewilderment of Stendhal's Fabrice on the battlefields of Waterloo. As often, he brought up the retreat. He writes, 'It was night. The last sections of the main column were far ahead, and had taken with them orderlies, who were left at the various crossroads to point the way they had chosen. It was this which induced Captain Mosso, who had kept near me, to say after a few hundred paces that, as he couldn't see or hear anything ahead, he thought we must have lost our way. We were in a place where several roads branched off in different directions. I halted my men, drawing them up to face Arezzo, and sent scouts along several of the possible roads: one of them soon caught up with the column. At last we emerged from the sunken track on to a wooded plateau, where a part of the cavalry had already dismounted, who told us that the camp was being pitched there. I looked for the General, but found neither him nor his men: instead I came across an orderly who had instructions to lead us on.

'While we were remounting I heard some heavy firing from the city, which was about 1000 yards away. I couldn't understand what this was at all; the best course seemed to me to climb up a small hill near the road, and get ready to confront the enemy. We wouldn't be able to make use of the cavalry here, so I told them to follow the column, at the same time sending a report to the General. Tricked by the darkness and by echoes, I then thought that the enemy had attacked the vanguard of the main body – or that Garibaldi had turned back and was approaching the city in order, perhaps, to take the main Anghiari road. I commanded my men to keep the strictest silence and held them in readiness to surprise the enemy, should they be pursuing us. Nothing at all could be seen. The flashes of gunfire illuminated the walls of the city for a split second, then everything was back to pitch darkness. Here and there a spent cannon-ball fell at our feet. At last the firing stopped altogether. I rode on with Captain Mosso behind the column: then suddenly my companion hurtled on to the road with his horse down from an eight-foot wall, only then noticing that the wall was there at all . . . my own horse reared just in time, otherwise I should have followed him. A few hundred yards further on we met Migliazzi who had been posted there by the General to show us the way (which he himself had avoided, because it passed so close underneath the walls of the city) . . . the General couldn't explain the reason for the firing; he thought that I had attacked Arezzo; or else that the Austrians had caught up with me . . . if the Austrians *had* pursued us with a few companies, we should probably have had to continue marching all night.'

As it was, they bivouacked, astride the road that leads over the Scopetone pass, near the watershed of the Arno and the Tiber.

'Do you think we might explore uphill, to the church of St Peter?'

'Or downhill? There's something marked Casa Nuova. More promising.'

We had arrived at the top early in the morning, after our night in Arezzo. Although Scopetone is not a very high pass – little more than 1500 feet – there is a suggestion, at the top, of leaving one country for another; lying behind us were the wide valleys, vineyards, villas, douce lowland prosperity, lying before us a series of wild, afforested hills and ridges, isolated villages by the side of whose every house logs are stacked against hard winters. A border is perceptibly crossed, even although this is still Tuscany. Ten minutes downhill, and we came to the first bridge over the Cerfone, the brown waters of the stream glistening through the green of pine trees and, beyond that, a glimpse of glades carpeted with spring flowers, gentians, aconites, crocuses – although precisely which flowers were responsible for the haze of blue I was never to know; for here the road winds steeply downhill and the valley of the Cerfone broadens out for a while, and pleasant meadows reach down to what had now become quite a respectable stretch of water, running level with the bank, and forming deep pools.

'Somewhere near here, do you think, they took their midday rest?'

'I think I shall just lie down, and put my feet in the water, while you peel me an orange.'

Hoffstetter saw the main body leave at two o'clock in the morning, in dead silence, and waited for some time before following with the rearguard. At noon the General did indeed halt by the shady bank of the Cerfone, and after reconnoitring decided that they could afford to rest – but not for long. He feared that the Austrians might be upon them at any moment, so that although the men ate the little white bread they still had left over, they did not risk slaughtering any oxen, in case there was no time to cook them.

Poor Hoffstetter! Until the dreadful night of confusion around Arezzo he had been in perfect health. But now he had begun to suffer from a terrible headache. Keeping in the saddle became a torment. To make it worse, the sun beat down 'like lead' into the narrow valley. Understandably, he has nothing more to say about what must have been an unendurable afternoon except that 'towards seven, we reached Monterchi, near the confluence of the Rivers Cerfone and Sovara'.

But before that, about one and a half miles upstream, there must be told the story of the rich peg-leg priest, living in the big house at Le Ville.

XVI

Citerna

(23-26 July)

NOT, LIKE THE GARIBALDINI, having spent an intermediate night on top of the rocky pass of Scopetone, I'm afraid that we decided that to walk all the way from Arezzo to the next habitable stage, Citerna, was a little too arduous. Without having Hoffstetter's excuse of a headache, we succumbed to the temptation of a bus for a portion of the journey, down the long valley darkened by threats of storm, and found ourselves alighting, and buying a picnic at Le Ville, small straggling town on the main road to Borgo San Sepolcro, at midday. Gluttony succeeded indolence. There was no need to follow the army's example by confining ourselves to a ration of white bread. The small grocer's shop sold us ham, cut into the thinnest of slices and laid out delicately in echelons on greaseproof paper, artichoke hearts, olives, wine.

'I think we have bought so much that we can reasonably ask him to show us – even take us – to the Villa Guadagni, the rich priest's house.'

'So long after? What makes you suppose it will still have the same name?'

But names of houses can be very long-lasting, and I was pretty sure that the imposing grey house almost opposite the grocer's shop, relics of a frieze showing beneath its eaves, was the one we were looking for.

'You *bullied* him into saying it was.'

'But you must agree that he said it very well might be. And it's certainly the largest and oldest house in the village now.'

Here, anyway, is the story, as recounted by Magherini-Graziani, the historian of Città di Castello, writing in 1896:

'At Le Ville there is one grand house, a kind of *palazzo*, called Villa Guadagni. Here there lived, in those days, a priest called Alberti, a nobleman by birth, talented, learned – and a passionate hunter. Hearing that Garibaldi was fast approaching the town on the way from Arezzo, all the inhabitants were terrified, as rumour had it that the Garibaldini ransacked everything and were no respecters of persons. None was more terrified than Alberti, both because he was a priest and because he was rich – and also because he had a wooden leg which would have made it very hard for him to run away, if he had had to. A nasty situation. Time was pressing and a decision had to be taken. Alberti summoned his household and addressed them: "If they come and ask for me, you must all tell them the same story, that the master is in bed because he has had to have a leg amputated. Be very careful all to say the same thing."

'As soon as he heard that the Garibaldini were approaching, he shut the windows of his room and went to bed, and in the room next to him put one of his most trusted servants (as he would have done had he been really ill) to attend to his master's needs. It was the evening of July 23rd. The Garibaldini went from house to house to fix up their food and lodging as best they could; and since the priest Alberti had the grandest house, the press of officers and soldiers round it was greater than anywhere else. Confusion reigned for quite a while, and it was only after midnight that the servants finally managed to shut the door. No sooner had they bolted it than there was a loud knocking. Looking out of a window they asked, "Who is it?" In reply, a loud, commanding voice, "Open up, for God's sake." Without waiting to be told twice they opened the door, and ran up the stairs, to attend to the lights. Three senior officers were before them. One of them asked, "Where's Dom Antonio?"

'The servant who had opened the door put on a very sad face and stuttered, "Poor man, he's in bed, ill."

'"What's wrong?"

'"He's had a leg cut off."

'"By this time it ought to have grown again."

'At the top of the stairs, the officer once again asked the servant – who was dumb with terror, with a face as white as a sheet – "Where is he, then?"

'"In bed."

'"Take me to him."

'"I'll go and tell him."

'The poor fellow staggered into his master's room, and reappearing, said, "Gentlemen, please come in."

'The officer who was enquiring after Dom Antonio rushed

forward, bounded into the room and jumped on the bed, and exclaimed to the priest – terrified out of his wits as the officer hugged and kissed him – "Don't you recognize me, you old rascal?"

'Dom Antonio was so bewildered that he couldn't find his breath.

'"Don't you remember me? That great hunt we had at – oh what year was it? – at Todi?"

'"So then . . . you're . . ."

'"Ciceruacchio!"

'As can be imagined, the scene changed at once: Dom Antonio and Ciceruacchio jumped off the bed and embraced and hugged each other, in a great state of emotion, in front of the servant who stood there, lamp in hand, completely bewildered.

'The two companions of Ciceruacchio were Giuseppe Garibaldi and one of his aides-de-camp.

'Dom Antonio did his best to make up for his original welcome by every expression of friendship and kept his guests in his house all night.'

Hunting does make strange bedfellows; but, all the same, this tale of the rich, aristocratic priest embracing the Roman pothouse-keeper, the man who had done more than anyone else to make the Pope's last days in Rome a misery by such threatening antics as throwing cardinals' hats into the Tiber – and whose son had assassinated the Pope's minister – does make very curious reading. Yet it has the ring of truth.

'Showing the Italian talent for improbable friendships?'

'Like communist leaders circulating in grand Roman society, you mean?'

I had brought with me a précis of the story, and used the paper as a form of plate for my bread, as we ate our picnic after climbing up the gentle slopes of Citerna's western hill. It had been a pleasant walk from Le Ville of less than two hours, part of it along the grassy track of a disused narrow-gauge railway, sleepers long since pulled up. A broad meadow, oxen grazing in one corner, swept upwards to young oak-woods; at its green margin, in the shelter of one of the larger trees, we rested after lunch, comfortable in the knowledge that we were now less than half an hour away from our goal.

But there was to be a diversion. We were now within a few yards of the drive which leads, along a southern spur, to what was the monastery of the Capuchins, and is today restored as a country villa, delightful with lawns, orchards, a paddock full of palomino horses tossing their manes, and, most interesting of all for my purpose, the bower where Anita and the General rested. Here beneath laurels trained on a trellis a monument was erected a month after Garibaldi's death to record for ever 'this dolorous episode in his pitiable Odyssey'.

In its shade Hoffstetter, too, enjoyed a short rest, writing afterwards, 'My indisposition, which turned into a sort of gastric 'flu, got so much worse towards evening that I was compelled to abandon the beautiful pergola in the garden of the monastery, and retire to one of the filthy cells in the cloister.' Though I am sure that Hoffstetter never complained openly, his departure must have made it more restful for the others.

Belluzzi, on his travels, was so enchanted by the sweet aspect of these gardens that he wrote, '. . . There is in the air such peace, melancholy, magical stillness! I walked among these grounds, enclosed by long rows of vines, and by green orchards. I saw the bower under which Garibaldi and Anita rested . . . Following the ways which Garibaldi took, I have had occasion more than once to observe how the places of rest, and the positions in which his tent was pitched are – quite apart from their good strategic sense – also the most beautiful ones, breathing a sweet and gentle poetry.'

Romantic excess? It can be forgiven in these surroundings. A similar note is struck in Magherini-Graziani's account of the deputation from Città di Castello who waited upon him in these gardens. For a moment I seem to catch, in Garibaldi's comportment, a melancholy echo of Richard III in the field before Bosworth. Ugo Bassi brought the men, who had largely come out of curiosity, up to the General:

'They went past a file of soldiers, entered a wood, and came to a small pergola. There was the General seated on a rock. He wore the red shirt, trousers of white leather with stripes of gold, high riding boots, white cloak, hat of black felt with a great black feather; and in his gold-striped belt was a small dagger, in a sheath of red velvet, with a handle of gold, ornamented with precious stones. Next to him was his wife, pale as death, who was eating walnuts which she had cracked on the rock she sat upon. As soon as he caught sight of his visitors the General rose, placing both his hands before him on the pommel of his sabre. Ugo Bassi spoke, "General, let me present to you the citizens of Città di Castello who will give you all the intelligence you may need."

'"Listen well," said Garibaldi. " First of all I must tell you one thing. If you mean to come with me, to enlist in my army, dismiss any such thought from your heads. I am surrounded on all sides, and I do not know what road will give me free passage. My army is melting away. I do not know how things will end."

'One of the deputation answered, "General, we have not come to enlist with you, only to salute you . . ."

'"I thank you. How far is Città di Castello from Citerna?"

'"About eight miles."

'"I know that the men of your city are good. Should I come among you, will I be received well, or ill? Will I find provisions for my men for a few days?"

'"Most of our people are good, I assure you. If you come you will be received with joy, for the partisans of the Pope are few, and will not dare to show their faces."

'Garibaldi did not reply and seemed lost in thought. Then Ugo Bassi said, "Gentlemen, the General is tired and needs rest; with your permission, it would be best to let him be now."

'All this time Garibaldi had been standing up – although he had been begged more than once to sit down. Now he shook hands with each of his visitors, taking his leave with indescribable courtesy. His last words were, "This time things have gone ill, but the blood which was shed in Rome will bear fruit, and I trust that in ten years' time at the most, Italy will be free. Courage and farewell."'

Like the inquisitive visitors from Città di Castello, we left the pergola'd garden, and walked back along the ridge, on to the road that curves up to Citerna. Unlike them, however, we did not find the town deserted, all the inhabitants fled in panic. In Garibaldi's day, even the butchers had vanished, having gone to Urbania on the pretext of attending a fair. Provisions were hard to come by, only wine was in good supply.

Our experience was very different, I am glad to say. We circled the walls, admiring the well-kept gardens which ornament the edges of this neat and prosperous town: the beds of geraniums, great pots of trailing roses set on stone walls: pine trees well spaced in small parks: grass, cut but not close-cropped, with wooden benches placed to look east to the high Apennines, south to the round hill of Monterchi, west up the long valley, towards the distant, misty pass over which we had just come.

Citerna is not large. Ten minutes' walk round the walled

perimeter brought us back to where we had started. This was by a new, low, dark-red hotel, set discreetly into the hill a little way beneath the encircling wall. In the red-tiled courtyard of the Sobaria there was a single Jaguar, with a Roman number plate.

'It looks too smart for us. Our boots . . .'

'We could walk through the town, and try to find a humbler establishment.'

We had some coffee in the tiny central square, within earshot of a three-tiered fountain, which splashed into a pool full of goldfish. But the inn, where we should properly have stayed, turned out to have been destroyed by an earthquake over half a century ago – in 1917. On the site where it stood a memorial, saved from its ruins, reads:

> This humble hostelry
> Welcomed in July 1849
> Giuseppe Garibaldi and his Anita
> The Commune of Citerna
> At its own expense, and with offerings
> Places this memorial
> Adding no further word
> So as not to spoil the eloquence
> Of so great a memory.

'Admirably modest inscription.'

'We could leave our rucksacks here, and brave the hotel that's still standing.'

The doors of the Sobaria opened on to an airy space, agreeably and casually furnished. Some wicker chairs, with coffee-coloured cushions, stood on tiled floors, by windows which looked, over the tops of pine trees, towards the setting sun. There was an air of quiet, of well-bred lack of ostentation. The bar was unattended, except for a friendly spaniel, dragging its lead.

'They can't all have *fled*, surely, in panic?'

'I don't know. At least we're not wearing feathers in black felt hats.'

But with what charm and kindness we were soon to be welcomed! The restaurant, so the proprietress apologized, was shut on Mondays. But perhaps we would be her guests for dinner?

It was indirectly through Signora Santucci's suggestions that, when the time came to leave this most engaging of hotels, I was to learn about the miracle of the sword of the statue of the archangel St Michael, patron saint of Citerna. That is, it was she who insisted that I must not fail to visit the library of Città di Castello; and it was while photocopying some pages of books found there that I met the estimable theological professor Dom Antonio Minciotti, from whom, a few weeks later, I was to receive a bundle of manuscripts copied from the Diocesan archives, together with the caveat that the miracle should not, perhaps, be taken too seriously. But as an illustration of the very understandable attitude of the Religious towards the General, he thought it was not without interest. I noticed that he had underlined the words *iniquo* and *detestabile* on the second page of the Deposition.

DEPOSITION

Of the miracle that happened in the venerable
Monastery of St Elizabeth of the Third Order
Of St Francis in the land of Citerna . . . by means
Of the small statue of St Michael Archangel,
On the occasion when the Piedmontese General
Giuseppe Garibaldi, fleeing from Rome, passed
Through and ravaged the said land in the days
From the 24th to 27 July 1849
 To the greater glory of God and of the glorious
Prince of the celestial hierarchy St Michael,
Protector of this land . . . the undersigned
Vicar, at his own expense, reclothed the small
Wooden statue of the Archangel . . . with a cloak
Of red silk, a small silver sword and other
Reverend ornaments . . . On the 8th of May of this
Year the statue, thus reclothed and reverently
Adorned, was taken from the monastery and exposed
To public veneration in the church of the Holy
Sacrament with due pomp . . . the Festival over,
The statue was brought back to the monastery
And given to the care of Sister Boni, who placed
It in the cell of the Mother Abbess . . . The veneration
Accorded to the statue of the first of the
Archangels by all the Religious grew ever more

In zeal when it was learnt that the iniquitous
Army of the detestable General Garibaldi was
Approaching from neighbouring Tuscany . . . known
By the stories bruited by his followers here
In this town of Citerna for the dissolution,
Violence, outrages, profanations, thieveries
And bloody slaughters which these infamous
Hordes committed in the Eternal City – and
Wherever they went – and which it makes us
Shudder to recall . . . At dusk on the evening
Of July 24 it was learnt that the town was
Invaded and occupied by that numerous band
Of ruffians, and the Monastery was surrounded
By them and they threatened to enter it
Immediately by force. At this sight, and
In the face of these threats, the timorous
Lambs of the Lord, terrified by the fear of
Seeing their cloister violated . . . and surrounded
By those monsters of Hell . . . far from any hope
Of human aid, and trusting in the mercy and
Omnipotence of God and in the patronage of the
Most holy Mary . . . addressed themselves more
Fervently than ever to their Archangel St Michael
With incessant prayers. All that night, without
Rest, the Religious prayed incessantly . . . so great
Was their trust in the Archangel that, when they
Gathered in the inmost places to be out of hearing
Of the blasphemous clamour outside, they took with
Them the statue, regarding it as their safeguard,
Their one unassailable bulwark. At dawn on July 25
One of those villains presented himself at the parlour
Of the monastery, and demanded with threats of force
A length of red damask, for making into a cloak
Similar to those they wear . . . two of the Religious
Conferred with each other and Sister Boni and decided
To unclothe the statue which they venerated and hide
The clothes to keep them safe, out of the hands of those
Treacherous thieves. To ease and hasten the undressing,
They thought first to remove the silver sword, held
In the statue's right hand. First Sister Boni loosened

A ribbon by which it was tied, and when it was free
She took the sword by its handle to pull it out from
The sheath but . . . however hard she tried she could not
Do it, was not able to move it even by a fraction.
Amazed, she called the Choral Sister Veronica, who came
Smiling in disbelief . . . but all *her* efforts were in vain
Too. The sisters looked at each other in amazement
And ran through the monastery crying, 'Miracle!
Miracle of our St Michael Archangel, who means to
Defend us. All the sisters gathered one after the
Other to hear the cause of these cries . . . When Sister
Boni explained they recited Pater Nosters and Aves . . .
Then all tried again and again to draw the sword but
Not one succeeded in moving it by one inch. Holy joy
Now took hold of all the sisters, as though certain
Of the protection of their Archangel, and they
Redoubled their prayers with ever greater fervour . . .
Especially when they learnt that the Man of Iniquities
General Garibaldi, with his detestable band of evil-doers
Were abandoning Citerna and proceeding towards Città di
Castello . . .

But this was a false dawn; for soon they were to hear that the
General had been rebuffed by an Austrian vanguard, and was
proposing to come back to Citerna, and to defend it. All their terrors
returned. Then four of the 'infamous band' climbed over the walls
of the orchard, one officer entered the parlour of the monastery, and
roamed the ground floor; another one even succeeded in breaking
into the cell of the abbess, who was sick, and threatened her when
he was told there was no money in the monastery chest. Finally,
after Garibaldi left them in peace the curious story of the miracle
closes:

Thus it was that all the Religious just as though
Moses had crossed the Red Sea with his miraculous
Army, rose in joy and offered misericordias to God,
And hymns of thanks to their Saint Archangel, for
Their deliverance from so many perils, in comparison
With so many inhabitants of Citerna, who had seen
Their cafés sacked, substance robbed, lives threatened . . .

The final proof of this miracle was given to Sister
Alberti who early on the morning of 27 July betook
Herself to the statue and no sooner did she touch
The silver sword than it moved. Thinking she was
Deceived she called Sister Clare who at once and
Easily drew the dagger from its sheath, to the
Marvel and amazement of all the Religious . . .

This is little more than a précis of the original deposition, which
runs to ten pages. Many redoubled prayers have been omitted,
many execrations of Garibaldi have been watered down. That the
Archangel St Michael, whose sword is used for chasing the wicked
from the gates of Heaven down to their proper habitation in Hell,
should have chosen to keep it sheathed, in symbolic readiness to
chase Garibaldi from the convent of Citerna, is fair enough; but the
authorities of the Church, following their tradition of caution and
delay, declined to authenticate the miracle, to the considerable
disappointment of the vicar of the day.

Citerna, as can be seen, is rich in recorded memories of the
General's disturbing passage. On our visit to the Commune,
however, the secretary apologized to us for the lack of official
archives: earthquake and fires had done their work. Except . . . from
the top of a bookcase he brought down and dusted a framed
montage of a dozen or more *buoni* or coupons, issued by the army
against requisitions of horses and provisions, and later redeemed by
the unfortunate council. In some of their corners appeared the
signature of Hugh Forbes, Colonel commanding the Second
Legion: precise, spiky English handwriting set beneath the frank of
the defunct Republic 'DIO E POPOLO'. How carefully the seal had
been preserved amongst the paraphernalia of the wandering army,
for all that no one could have supposed it any longer to have real
authority!

Before we left, we toured the bastions for one last time, hoping
to discover the embrasure, or at least guess the position, where
the precious cannon was pointed at the hill of Monterchi, one and a
half kilometres distant. About 2000 Austrians were reckoned to
have arrived here from Arezzo, by the time of the General's
departure. Although they could easily have made life most
uncomfortable for the Garibaldini, they preferred to observe and to
wait as the net grew ever tighter. Patrols from Citerna rode down

across the valley, and up beneath the walls, shouting taunts, calling the Austrians MANGIAZUCCHE and SEGONI.

'Why is it so insulting to be called a pumpkin-eater?'

'I can't imagine. SEGONI, though, is more obviously rude. "Big-cocks" or something like that.'

In any case, may the patron saint of Citerna be thanked for the avoidance of any serious engagement, any bombardment by either side! Cannon-balls rocketing to and fro these twin hills might well have fallen on the chapel in the valley between, where the pregnant Madonna of Piero della Francesca silences the visitors who come to pay her homage. Guarded by two attendant angels who hold back the curtain-flaps of the pavilion in which she stands, she points with the gracile fingers of one hand to the narrow slit in her swelling blue dress, and to the burden she carries; and she imposes an unalterable calm. Tumult is far, far away.

On the morning of our departure we decided to walk eastwards across the wide, tobacco-growing valley of the Tiber to Borgo San Sepolcro, and to cross the Sovara by a small bridge near a farmstead called Atena. This was more or less in the track of Garibaldi's night march of July 26th, though exactly which ford he crossed is uncertain. Was it here that the fat monks (more of whom he had taken hostage in Citerna to prevent their informing upon his movements) waded and wallowed and floundered so? What is certain was the amazement which the army felt at not being pursued. Not a single shot was fired that night. Hoffstetter was very disappointed.

'I had remained with the rearguard, which marched warily, on the alert for an attack . . . I could hardly keep in the saddle, I felt so weak, more dead than alive. But I wanted to be at hand, in case there was a fight – because I was convinced that then I should return to life.'

I suppose those are the sentiments of the true soldier. But my own preference, if I had to return to life from Hoffstetter's disease, would be to rest in a dappled clearing, such as the one we found to picnic in. Italian rivers and streams, especially in low-lying parts, can often be sad, muddy, shallow affairs, their banks unkempt, littered by torn plastic bags trailing on brambles. But the Sovara, on the morning we came to Atena, was a delight. Clear brown water ran over pebbles, here and there swirling into miniature whirlpools, as in a north-country trout-stream. Banks sloped down on to small beaches of sandy, alluvial soil. A broad, grassy path, unscarred by tractors, ran along the western side of the stream, occasionally opening out into glades. Best of all, both river and path were shaded by rows of poplars and alders, alive with bird-song, so that the waters ran and danced beneath one long tunnel of burgeoning green.

After this Arcadian interlude, the rest of our walk, towards the shingly shores of the Tiber itself, was in drab contrast. Sunshine gave way to slanting rain. We passed isolated, gaunt farmhouses where grey plaster had peeled from the walls and sometimes truncated the names of the properties, printed in bold black across the front. We skirted farmyards littered with rusty machinery, where hungry-looking dogs, kept on running-wires, roamed and snarled and barked. Yet the earth itself is rich and well-cultivated, even if so many of the large buildings are tumbledown; rural depopulation, it seems, rather than poverty is responsible for the air of neglect.

Nearer to San Sepolcro, we were not sorry when a small Fiat stopped and its driver insisted we should get in. I was glad, when he left us at the door of the museum, that we had talked, during the brief two or three miles, of Piero della Francesca and the Resurrection, rather than of Garibaldi and kidnapped monks; for I noticed (but only on saying goodbye) that there was a crucifix on the car-key ring and that our benefactor was a priest.

{XVII}
Bocca Trabaria
(27-28 July)

STRICTLY SPEAKING, we should not have ventured into San Sepolcro at all. By July 26th Austrian troops, coming from Arezzo *via* Anghiari, had occupied the town, barring any possible attempt by Garibaldi to march north up the valley of the Tiber. For the moment, however, we abandoned military considerations in favour of the claims of Piero della Francesca. I don't think any excuse is needed, although if it were I could claim that troops from Rome are present, even if asleep, in his magnificent fresco of the Resurrection. The four centurions, slumped round the tomb, convey boredom, indifference, drowsiness, the everlasting lot of the common soldier. The figure of the risen Christ, standing with one leg placed up on the marble slab, holding in his right hand the banner, with its cross, against a background of pale skies and wintry trees, expresses not victory, not miracle, not I think even majesty: nothing so much as absolute and transcendant certainty – and a stillness, too, as though he contained all Time.

'Poor sentries.'

'Fortunately my experience – either of being one or guarded by one, is *nil*.'

One account of Garibaldi's own sentries puts the behaviour of his men in these parts in a very much better light than that in which they are seen during the tale of the miracle of the Archangel St Michael. Another local historian introduces it and describes it well:

'As in all things in this world, some see everything as grey, others as all red or black. One shouldn't therefore be surprised if, in reciting the various tales of his passage, there are those who speak of gallantry, courtesy and consideration; and those who speak only of thefts, destruction and outrage. Giuseppe Donnini, for example, writes, "Having a few Garibaldini in one's house, or simply applying to any of their officers, was enough to guarantee you against any disagreeable surprise. An old chemist had a pair of oxen taken from his farm – but upon complaining to his guests, he immediately had them given back to him. In my own house we had three officers staying, who were so good as to visit my old father during his last days, on his deathbed. They comforted him and treated him with every possible kindness, they put sentries at the door of the cellar to ensure good order, they never asked the reasons for my absences, they never glanced inquisitively into our rooms as they went up and down the stairs, and they never made a single joke that was less than polite to any of the maids, one of whom at that time was rather showy. And Ugo Bassi prevented any harassment or bad treatment of the nuns – indeed, with his *bonhomie*, was of some comfort to them."'

Ugo Bassi seems to be everywhere on the stage during those days of skirmishing to and fro in the valley of the Upper Tiber. But if the robust and jovial Barnabite priest comforted some, he terrified others out of their wits. Magherini-Graziani tells how one poor priest, Dom Amanzio, had been so terrified to learn that the Garibaldini were approaching Città di Castello that he fled, stumbled and fell into a fish-pond. Hauled out of it, he was taken dripping to Ugo Bassi, who had ridden to the town square to demand provisions for the army. Mistakenly asked why he had risked his life attempting to ford the Tiber, the poor man broke out into a terrible nervous giggle and collapsed to the ground, as though about to die. Ugo Bassi then asked him whether he had celebrated mass that morning. Dom Amanzio nodded, Bassi asked him what the gospel of the day said, and Dom Amanzio relapsed into more nervous giggles. At last Ugo Bassi said, 'I see you are feeble-minded' and after himself reciting the gospel, added this lecture, 'All Catholics together form the flock, and the Pope is the supreme shepherd, after him came the bishops and then the other shepherds, the priests. The flock is obliged to follow the counsel of the shepherd and to obey him, but equally it is the duty of the shepherd to protect the flock from any danger that threatens it. You have not pondered what you read today, or you have not understood it; and thinking that we, followers of Garibaldi, have come to the city to commit who knows what crimes and outrages, you have to your shame fled in panic and abandoned the flock which, at whatever risk to your life, you ought to have defended. You have done badly, for we are not *cannibals* . . . Go home and get dry so as not to catch cold.'

The doctrine seems unexceptionable, even if Ugo Bassi's conduct does have less orthodox aspects. When he tried to requisition arms, for example, and was refused, he demanded at least to be taken to the armoury to see what the city possessed, and at the end of his visit he asked for, and was given, a couple of pistols. Distressed by the state of his trousers, which were torn to shreds, he was delighted to accept a pair of red ones, 'almost new', from an officer of the civic guard.

This was a period of the long march when people met old friends: first there was the peg-leg priest at Le Ville, and now at Città di Castello Bassi met another acquaintance who had helped him once to prepare the church at San Severino for festival. Preparations for festivals are still splendidly extravagant, as we were to witness ourselves that evening. For off a hill-road near San Sepolcro we came to an isolated chapel, which was not only decked inside with every kind of spring flower and with waxen lilies, but whose exterior, too, was embroidered with a myriad light bulbs. Wooden fences along the road leading to it were festooned with many-coloured baubles and bells and Chinese lanterns. An arch, especially erected for the festival at the entrance of the drive, was entwined with ivy, stalks of asparagus fern and plastic roses *ad majorem gloriam*. When darkness fell, there were to be fireworks. We waited. Rockets unloosed their diamond cascades of red and blue and green, to scatter and fall, light upon light, down towards the illuminated cross that stood upon the western porch of the church. Hundreds of feet beneath us even more lights twinkled, those of the cities of the plain, San Sepolcro and San Giustino and Città di Castello.

But the first occasion on which we had visited this church had been in the evening of our arrival in San Sepolcro, in order to reconnoitre possible ascents of the high Apennines the next day. We stood looking down on to the valley, and it was easy from this height to people it with toy soldiers – to re-enact, as in some nursery game, one or two incidents of Garibaldi's day.

'That time when *both* sides ran away, you mean?'

'I suppose that was a bit Gilbert and Sullivanish.'

A patrol of three Garibaldini on horseback had ridden south from Città di Castello. A hundred or so Austrians caught sight of them and supposing that the city was therefore safe in Garibaldi's hands (which it wasn't), took to their heels and fled back towards

Umbertide. The Garibaldini thought that the violent haste of the Austrians' movements was the prelude to pursuit; so themselves turned round, spurred their horses, and galloped back to the town. Not a shot was fired on either side.

However, there were one or two rather more bloodthirsty episodes. Poor Cipriano Angiolini had worked night and day as a spy for Garibaldi, bringing him news of the force who now surrounded him on all sides. Arrested near the Belvedere, that most beautiful, domed, brick-red edifice which overlooks Città di Castello, he was brought back into the town (which was now securely in Austrian hands) and tied fast to a manger in a stall, with his arms bound under his knees, 'trussed like a goat'. During the night of July 30-31st the troop who had taken him prisoner left town throwing him, bruised all over from his day's beating-up, on to a farm-cart. After a few miles he begged to be allowed to walk and permission was given. Clearly a man of great strength and desperation, he managed within a few minutes to seize a soldier's bayonet and laid about him to right and left 'transfixing as many Austrians as he could'. For all the fight that he put up, he was inevitably overpowered in the end, trussed up again, and shot 'towards Ave Maria'.

But the oddest incident of all concerns the map that failed to mark the main road. A Moderate historian, Carlo Corsi, writing in 1870, recalls the days in Florence when he heard, with alarm, hideous rumours of Garibaldi's army moving towards the Adriatic, committing outrages, spreading destruction wherever it went. Someone like himself, he said, who had ties of family or of interest in the hinterlands of the Marches felt bound to go to protect them. He set off with a friend, but near San Sepolcro aroused the suspicions of a patrol of Austrian hussars. However, an officer accepted a lift in his carriage and soon 'spread out a map of Tuscany on his knees, and pointed with a finger to all the roads along which Austrian columns were advancing. Garibaldi, he said, will be "chopped in pieces". But I saw that the map failed to show the new Ancona road that passes over the Apennines at the Bocca Trabaria, and I laughed and asked him where the map came from. From the general staff, he said. When he realized why I had laughed, instead of cursing the staff . . . he insisted that any such omission was quite impossible, because the Austrians always kept their maps up to date in every detail. "Oh, well," I said. "You'll soon see."'

The curious fact is that on our walk we carried an Austrian 1:86,400 map, published in 1850, which clearly shows the main road – completed, as it was, in 1840. Yet Corsi's tale rings true, and certainly helps to explain why the Austrians closed their pincers in such a negligent, leisurely fashion, letting their prey escape.

There may have been other reasons, too. Corsi tells of one exhausted Austrian captain who exclaimed, 'This devil will lead us all to Hell – or to Africa at the very least. He's another Abd-el-Kader' – referring to the desert chieftain. And he adds that the officers to whom he spoke were full of admiration for Garibaldi, thinking him to be a 'partisan' of extraordinary courage; and they didn't, in their hearts, want to come to grips with him, but hoped that he could find some loophole. The idea that a battle would be a useless massacre weighed heavily on those with most sense.

Before leaving Corsi, and following Garibaldi while he discovered the loophole and climbed over the high Apennines, it is worth quoting the Florentine historian's estimate of the local inhabitants' attitudes, too:

'Certainly they had no sympathy at all for the Austrians. But for Garibaldi – yes: though it was combined with the usual hope that he would hurry up and go away. His patrols scoured the country, taking horses ... To make sacrifices with no hope of advantage, for a cause that was already lost, did not appeal to these people. So they wished *bon voyage* to the brave condottiere and his band.'

Well, they left at dawn on July 27th, making very fair haste up the steep mountain road, only halting after three hours to kill and cook some of their oxen, and to rest. By seven in the evening they were at the top of the pass, about 3000 feet above sea level.

Here Hoffstetter took time to gaze down on to the column which was climbing up towards him, along the corkscrew road. I think he may have been inspired by the fast which succeeded his gastric 'flu – by hunger – for the vision brought out a burst of poetry in him. I shall quote the passage in full.

'The column wound its way slowly towards the summit in gigantic spirals, as though it was some great, beautiful snake. At its head, there rode Garibaldi by the side of his heroic wife, followed by his staff, distinguishable from afar by their white cloaks, played upon by the mountain breezes. Then came the lancers, the few survivors of Masina's gallant band, before whom on April 30th an entire battalion of the French had laid down their arms, who at

Velletri had fought like heroes, who on the steps of the Villa Corsini had lost their leader. Enviable death! Then came the volunteer cavalry, two by two, a long train of picturesque uniforms. Their hats with feathers, red shirts and arms of many different sorts (one section carried carbines and bayonets like dragoons) produced the most colourful, extraordinary effect. All the horses, nimble and sure-footed, climbed up on the ridge at a lively pace, puffing and snorting. Muleteers drove our beasts of burden before them – forty mules with dark-brown coats – goading them on with shouts, oaths, whips. Following them, a herd of white oxen with heavy horns, long and curved, picked their steps warily. Then there was a space, and after that the infantry. First, the three much-reduced cohorts of the former Italian Legion, led by the good Sacchi. From under their hats worn *alla calabrese* there looked out those same bronzed, bold faces which were the pride and joy of Garibaldi: a legion now down to nothing more than a mere guard of honour for the standard which was – yes – riddled with bullets, but still safe in our hands. Between this and the second legion four horses pulled our solitary, but nonetheless prized, cannon. Leading the second legion came Forbes and his young son, the two eccentric Englishmen in their summer suits, whose men were distinguished from the first legion by their light-grey tunics and their kepis. The Bersaglieri and the revenue guard brought up the rear, now numbering no more than a hundred men, sole representatives of those two most distinguished corps, the one with their uniforms of bright blue with red facings, the other with their well-known "*round hats*". What sorrow seized me now as those Bersaglieri drew near and, full of grief, I looked for my old companions-in-arms! Where is Manara? Where is Dandolo, Rozzat? Where Marosini? These relics of the army of the Republic who now climbed Mount Luna hardly came to 2000 men in all – and even these must soon vanish. And as though to add to my anguish, and make contrast with my melancholy, the sun was setting clear, and sending its last beautiful rays on the white, white rocks and on the fertile hills beneath.'

How very pardonable to indulge in remembrance and sentimental reflections when standing, looking westwards, on a high pass at sunset! But it is equally common to be brought down to earth by some petty irritation. Hoffstetter was no exception:

'The mountain air had refreshed me, and after three days of terrible pains I was feeling better. One quiet night would have restored me completely. So it was that, as soon as the column had arrived at the top of the pass, I retired to a nearby building, where the rearguard was quartered, and there found the bed I so longed for. But I was to be bitterly disappointed, because not only was I attacked by an entire army of pestilent insects, but on top of that, a cavalryman was brought in who had been wounded in the knee by a bullet, when on patrol. A crowd stood around near me, helping to extract it. Despite the morning frost I left the building, looking for a bit more rest in the open air.'

Mounted patrols always flanked the General's marches; and if the wounded cavalryman disturbed Hoffstetter's rest, he also provided an additional excuse – if any were needed – for our not following in the steps of the main body over the mountain. For we had no wish to climb on foot the tortuous zigzags of the familiar main road, well-marked on our map. Besides, the reconnaissance of the previous evening had satisfied us about the paths up from the village of Valdimonte. We had been encouraged, too, by a local innkeeper who had told us, 'You know it's the *old* road over the top? Roman coins were found in it a few years ago, by a farmer mending the stone walls.' He had come out from behind his bar, parted the bead curtains of the café and pointed, a little vaguely it's true, up the hill. Then he had added, 'It is a wonderful way when you get up on the ridge, with views north and south as far as Perugia and Trasimene. But be careful. You may get lost in the woods near the top.'

It isn't common, in these parts, to find a local inhabitant who can give advice to hill-walkers. Not, indeed, that he thought that our plan of following (more or less) in the footsteps of Garibaldi other than very peculiar indeed. His knowledge, for which we were grateful, stemmed from the more rewarding autumn days he spent on the mountain with his dogs and gun. (The thought of the bullet in the cavalryman's knee flitted across my mind.)

So the next morning we made a dawn start, and arrived by eight o'clock at the narrow-spired mountain church of Valdimonte, hard by a cemetery. From here we had the choice of a stony track, making steeply up the ridge, or a gentle incline northwards, along a gravel road, bordered by occasional apple and walnut trees, which led as far as a cluster of greystone farmhouses. This latter track we preferred. At a curve just before the hamlet, we came in sight of a walled vineyard, planted on a steep-sloping southern face.

'Very thin wine, surely, they'd get at this height?'

'I don't know. Perhaps we should stop and ask to sample some.'

But we were not tempted further to any such indulgence; for two barking dogs, and a bowed figure raising a stick either at us or at the dogs – it was not clear which – were the only signs of life. We passed underneath a lichened wall, blank-faced except for a single, tiny, iron-barred window high up; then crossed through an ageing orchard, many or most of whose fruit trees had moss growing on their trunks. At this hour of the morning it was a melancholy neighbourhood. At last we shut behind us a well-built wooden gate and emerged on to high, open pastureland. On the skyline above us we could make out white splodges, slowly moving, 'oxen with heavy curved horns, picking out their steps warily'.

'They are lucky not to be due for immediate slaughter, roasting and eating.'

'And we not to be kneecapped.'

We were now making excellent, uncrippled progress along turfed mountain tracks. A cattle-pool by whose margin we passed, was surprisingly clear, our reflections visible in its green waters, until a sudden jumping of frogs disobligingly rippled them. Beneath us, deep in the valley, another pool was fringed by poplars, and the vision of different greens, of grass and water and tree-bark and leaves, had a haunting mystery, depth and escape. No nettles, no lumps of sodden clay which a closer approach would doubtless have revealed, could be seen from our superior path.

Three mountain streams we should have crossed, by my estimate, before this path took a hairpin bend, to zigzag up to the ridge. At one of these we stopped, and drank the clear water which bubbled from a source by its side. But then – ah, classic temptation! – we failed to turn from our broad, easy, well-worn track, and found ourselves walking more or less on the level: in effect, towards the re-entrant of the small river Valdimonte, the rustle of whose pools and occasional waterfalls began to reach our ears. In time, we turned from the error of our way and scrambled up steep trackless country, dislodging rocks, pausing often for breath, until after half an hour or so, we reached the coveted ridge. The scramble had been arduous enough to allow us to pretend that we deserved the views which were now spread before us. Not, indeed, that they extended to the waters of Lake Trasimene. Mists still hung about several of the valleys and peaks; and the layers of hills and mountains, towards the Adriatic especially, looked black. Their faces were still in shade, the fitful sun could not reach them.

This was *not* one of those Italian views, background to the paintings of Piero, with blue skies, clear distances, reflections of white. What lay before us was brooding, changeable, frightening even, a vast empty Gothic landscape of fastnesses, crags and caverns – farmsteads built on spurs of hills arising out of lakes of mist and pretending to be castles – all the vocabulary of the picturesque.

Few pleasures can be compared with that of walking along the springy turf paths of high ridges on a cool morning: all the more so since not very much more effort seemed now to be called for. Dense woods still lay before us but already the inn on the summit of the pass (the Four Chimneys) was coming into sight – and not very high above us, either.

Our track forked at the entrance to the wood. One broad, leafy path pointed directly towards the four chimneys, which puffed a few inviting wisps of smoke. Breakfast seemed a mere half-hour away, or less. Navigation had been exemplary, fears of getting lost in the wood quite laughable.

'Wonderful things, these Swedish compasses. I'm allowing two degrees West for magnetic error this year.'

'We only have to follow our nose. I can almost smell the coffee already.'

We strode confidently along the muddy track, skirting a small landslide here, a fallen branch there. A few drops of rain through the canopy of leaves were agreeable, refreshing. But then the four chimneys gradually, mysteriously, began to loom higher over us than before. Nor did we seem to be getting any nearer to them. An optical delusion – or not?

'I'm getting worried. This path is leading downhill.'

'*Downhill?* What do you mean, downhill? It's still pointing straight at the chimneys. Don't be ridiculous. I could run all the way from here. Or gallop, if I had a horse.'

'Exactly, *downhill*!'

We consulted the map. Over-confidence on hill-walks brings retribution. It was clear we had once again succumbed to the scriptural temptation. The broad, easy path led to another re-entrant of the valley, rather than to the top of the pass.

'No time spent in reconnaissance is ever wasted. Who said that?'

'The General? I'm afraid he probably did no better than us.'

We retreated to the original fork. What we had to do was to skirt the other side, or brim, of Monte Antonio. For about twenty minutes we had the sheer bulk of its summit between us and our elusive goal. After that, a steep path of scree led us up to a low shoulder, on whose dimple was marked one of the head-springs of the Meta which, twinned with the Auro, debouches at Fano, as the famous River Metaurus.

'We should think of Hannibal, and the battle lower down, and elephants.'

'Hannibal! I am thinking of my breakfast.'

We took another compass bearing. Evidently we should now walk north for about seven minutes, then west for another seven minutes. I said, 'Don't worry. We are a quarter of an hour from your coffee at the most.' But soon the tone of the conversation deteriorated.

'Doesn't it strike you we are walking up and up and round and round? At this rate we'll be climbing to the top of the bloody mountain.'

'This is the path. Muddy, but definitely the path.'

'I shall go back.'

We went back. Another track promised better, following the contour. But soon it meandered into a bog, then petered out altogether. Between some thickets I caught sight of a slope which I recognized.

'Two minutes now. A year ago I distinctly remember having a picnic just over *there* – on our way to Florence.'

'I don't trust you any longer.'

The innocuous-looking beechwoods which clothe the top of the Apennines conceal – hereabouts anyway – dense thickets of thorn, and of other undergrowth which I did not bother to identify. Soon we were caught in them.

'"*Nel mezzo cammin della mia vita . . .*"'

'I'm much more than halfway through *my* life, thank you.'

It is a bad sign when walkers try to quote, accurately or not, the first few lines of the *Inferno*. Even worse was to follow.

'I can't get out of this scrub at all.'

'Crawl.'

'I am crawling.'

'Crawl lower.'

'Where are you?'

'I don't know.'

At last, clothes and temper both ragged, we sat down to an early lunch, rather than to a late breakfast.

But Hoffstetter, too, had had his petty irritations at the top of the Bocca Trabaria, so we were in a sense keeping faith with the Swiss Major, although he, poor fellow, had to wait until Mercatello, twelve or so miles on, before being consoled with food and wine.

XVIII

Sant'Angelo in Vado

(28-29 July)

SOME OF THE HIGH VALLEYS which branch from the road that leads down to the Adriatic, have nobler trees, and better-tended forestry, than the ones in whose thickets we had scrambled. The name of the pass 'Bocca Trabaria' literally means 'mouth of the beams'; and it was from the ancestors of these oaks, five centuries ago, that beams were taken for the roofs of St Peter's in Rome. Today, in timber yards by the side of the road, piles of beams, and logs of every size, are still stacked; and from autumn until early spring the noise of the sawmills punctuates the silence of the mountains. Mules, sleek-coated and incredibly strong, still totter down forestry paths, their spines and heads just visible above the loads lashed to their flanks. Here and there, blue trails of smoke between the trees still signal the presence of charcoal-burners and at one clearing close to the riverbank near Borgo Pace a quarter-acre of ground is for ever charred: black igloos of sticks dot the site and men whose faces are as black as miners coming from coal pits cover the fires, rake cinders, fill the large sacks. Theirs is a hard job, picturesque only to the onlooker, which has changed little if at all since Garibaldi's day: a story by one of his most distinguished lieutenants, Giuseppe Abba, tells how a fugitive from Napoleon's army, shivering on the ridges of the Apennines, found his way by following the giveaway wisps of smoke, down to the sanctuary of a charcoal-burner's cottage.

'With a beautiful dark-haired daughter, I hope.'

'To the General's taste? What *was* his taste in ladies?'

We had been briefly discussing the point during an excellent lunch at La Diligenza in Borgo Pace – a restaurant which stands on the site of the last staging-post before the ascent of the pass, over which we had come. The question arose because we had before us an account of the local historian who described Garibaldi's arrival in Mercatello (a little further on) with 'his Anita, a *most beautiful* Creole who wished always to be with him in his adventures'. *Bellissima* is a gallant exaggeration, I'm afraid. The historian insisted that Garibaldi was in a most affable mood during his brief stop in the town, although surely it must have been the affability of despair. He gave one of his precious cigars to a local man who had come to see him merely out of curiosity; and he had received, with expressions of great gratitude, a basketful of figs from the Prior, Count Marsili.

'*And* he was running short of cigars at this stage.'

'I think it's even more proof of affability to give effusive thanks for a rotten old basket of figs.'

But when he took leave of Count Marsili, he made a speech, another version of which we had already read in Citerna.

'Tomorrow, citizens of Mercatello, you will once again be slaves – but, my friends, we shall meet again in ten years' time.'

In ten years' time, so he used to remind his listeners, his Battalion of Hope, composed of boys between ten and fifteen years old, would be able to fight as grown men for the liberty and unity of Italy. Patience!

But now his men had barely three hours to enjoy their rest and refreshment. A little after midday news came from the scouts who had been sent forward, that detachments of Austrians were advancing from Urbania towards St Angelo in Vado. They realized once again that they were hemmed in, since they had no doubt that the other Austrian forces, from Arezzo, were hard on their heels.

The drum called the men to arms, and the General galloped with the first squadron of cavalry he was able to muster to St Angelo, five miles away. Battle was in the air. A second squadron was saddled up, and followed as soon as possible. Two cohorts of infantry, then, at a distance of 1000 yards. Forbes, with his Second Legion, was left behind in Mercatello, ready to face the pursuing enemy expected any minute.

Those dispositions made, Hoffstetter, fully recovered from his gastric 'flu, galloped after Garibaldi to St Angelo. He found the town in turmoil. 'No sooner had the General expressed his wish that the infantry (on the point of arriving) should be refreshed with wine than the burghers brought it out on the streets in enormous containers – indeed in whole barrels.'

Meanwhile the cavalry reconnoitred beyond the city. They

found that several companies of Austrian riflemen had taken up position some 2000 yards to the east. It is here that a steep spur runs down to the valley-bed, leaving a very narrow passage – along which the road runs to Urbania – between the foot of the hill and the bank of the Metaurus. They could not tell how many of the enemy might be drawn up on the far side of the strait.

Later that afternoon Garibaldi ordered his men to close columns and prepare for battle. He rode with Anita to the front of the column, resolved to force a passage. But, just in time, he learnt that, after all, a way of escape lay open – a rough mule-track that winds north over the hills into the valley of the Foglia. Another loophole! He ordered his staff to wait on a hillock nearby, and accompanied by a single lancer, rode a little way along this track, to try to steal a sideways look at the enemy position.

By dusk his men were encamped between St Angelo and the strait with the exception of fifty men under Major Migliazzi who were left in the town, and a few pickets posted back on the Mercatello road. In addition, one company was put on guard at the entrance to the strait, and another on the track that led over the hills to the Foglia – which they hoped to take tomorrow.

As Hoffstetter says, their position was far from comfortable, threatened as it was both from east and west (and possibly north, too). Had the General not had such a pressing need of supplies from the town, he would have preferred to strike up into the hills before nightfall. But he feared that in the desolate country ahead which they must now traverse, they would find '*il gran nulla*' – the great nothing.

Two bloody scuffles early next morning – the only fights of any consequence since leaving Rome – were the sorry consequences of his decision. The first disaster fell when a body of twenty lancers made another attempt to reconnoitre the road towards Urbania. The Austrians drew back as the platoons, foolhardily, rode forward. No sooner were they in the jaws of the strait than they fell victim to a well-laid ambush. Riflemen fired down from the wooded slopes. The lancers' horses were shot from under them. Many of them escaped, but five men were taken prisoner – two of them French – then shot out of hand.

Their bones now lie interred, under a patch of ground near to where they fell. A stone monument, laurel-wreathed, marks the spot. The inscription on it reads:

Sant' Angelo in Vado (28-29 July)

On the plain of the Metaurus
There fell as warriors
Overwhelmed by force of numbers,
By Austrian guile, by Austrian lead
Defenders of Rome, at the close of their march.
History has not kept their names
But the People have honoured them
With the name of – ITALY
And have preserved their memory
Recalling the last curse, and the last prayer
Of the unknown martyrs.

We had walked from St Angelo to the place of ambush, along a pleasant road lined with lime trees. Here, too, we inspected a rusting field-gun, and patted its barrel. For the small grove, planted with pines, now serves also as a memorial to the city's fallen of both World Wars; the five Garibaldini overshadowed by greater slaughter, on other fields.

On our way to and from the grove and the city we counted our steps, under our breath, occasionally stopping and sitting on milestones to let each other catch up.

'I make it 600 so far. Or was it 650?'

'300. Ah, 300 double paces. All right. Twenty-five more.'

For the rough track which Garibaldi took over the hills, according to Hoffstetter, left the main road exactly 1400 paces east of the city; this was what we wished to reconnoitre before our own walk the next day. Fortunately an old man, carrying a scythe, was able to confirm the results of our laborious pacing. Most of the names have not changed over the last century, and we became satisfied that we had correctly identified the church and farmhouse from which the baggage train started out at ten o'clock on July 29th.

This start was much later than Garibaldi would have wished. The horses had been taken down to the Metaurus to water, section by section, and that took time. But with the enemy so close, they could not afford to let all the cavalry remain *hors de combat* at the same time.

At last the First Legion set out, all the advance posts except the company guarding the strait were called in, and Forbes was on the point of ordering his Second Legion to march – when Major Migliazzi out of breath, without his beret and followed by only a handful of his men, galloped out of St Angelo and, exhausted, told the tale of the bloodiest disaster that had yet befallen the expedition.

A small band of Austrian hussars had suddenly appeared from nowhere and, sabres held high above their heads, charged at full tilt down the main street of St Angelo (now the Corso Garibaldi). The fifty horse in the town were caught utterly by surprise. They had lost touch with the picket on the Mercatello road. No guard had been placed on either of the gates. Their horses were still unsaddled. The men were wandering in and out of their billets or still eating their breakfast.

In no time at all the Austrians had occupied both gates of the town. Flight was impossible, save over the walls and through the houses. The massacre began. A Captain Orlandi of Perugia, thrown by his horse and surrounded by several hussars with sabres drawn, surrendered and was, seconds afterwards, shot dead. Another Garibaldino with one hand all but severed, crept under an aqueduct and dragged himself to a mill: the miller called a *vet* and an operation saved his life. Poor Captain Jourdan, a Frenchman, was attacked by hussars while saddling his horse. He refused to surrender, drew a pistol and killed one of his assailants, and immediately had the back of his head cleft to the bone, from ear to ear. Then he was shot. A bullet went through the lobe of his right ear. He fell in a pool of blood and, not surprisingly, was left for dead.

By some extraordinary feat of will, he managed to make his way out of town. At the camp, dripping with blood from his sabre-gash, he was met by an astounded Hoffstetter who could not believe his eyes. How was Captain Jourdan still alive, let alone standing on his feet? Yet he remained perfectly upright and gave his report in a good, clear voice. Since the doctors and stretchers had already gone forward, Hoffstetter's only course was to seat him, as best he could, on his own horse. That, however, he was able to bear for only a few minutes, after which he collapsed and four men somehow carried him onwards. A doctor was found, who gave his opinion that he could not possibly survive with a wound like that, especially in the dreadful heat of the day. At last he was put on a stretcher and borne, in slow stages, by eight men all the way to Macerata Feltria.

Here he was left behind in a friendly house. But his ordeal was not over. After the Garibaldini had moved on again, the Austrians

made a house-to-house search, found him and dragged him –
dressing him only in his bloody shirt – before the Austrian
commander, Count Stadion. Under interrogation about the
whereabouts of his fellow-soldiers, he replied only 'You must know
that I do not have to answer that. You know the rules of war.' So
impressed was Count Stadion by the Captain's fortitude that he set
him free with orders that two sentries should be placed outside the
door of his small inn, and that a black flag should fly there, to
indicate that it was now 'a hospital'. Captain Jourdan recovered and
emigrated to America.

At last, exclaims Professor Fini, the historian of St Angelo, one
can find a generous Austrian gesture to report! Indeed: for it does
seem that the Austrians behaved here with calculated brutality.
There is evidence that the citizens were forced to witness the
spectacle of the slaughter in the main streets *pour encourager les
autres*. Some closed their eyes, or hid in their houses. Later, others
took in the wounded soldiers, disguised them at the risk of reprisals
and helped them escape. Only one man, a cobbler, betrayed a
Garibaldino and 'he died mad'.

The Austrians' own account of this episode to some extent bears
out these reports of savagery. 'The confusion of the rebels was
complete, the terror was general, and their flight so precipitous that
in the barren rocky mountains they nearly died of hunger. *Some
executions in Sant' Angelo made them realize the fate that awaited
them*, and the certainty of punishment gave them wings to flee over
rocky ridges and precipices at breakneck speed.' (My italics)

But here in St Angelo the General himself suffered a wound even
more bitter than that inflicted by the fiasco of these two bloody
engagements. Treachery, a stab in the back, must always be more
dispiriting than the loss of a battle, and, in the night before the
hussars' mad charge through the city, Garibaldi's old South
American comrade-in-arms Bueno decamped, carrying with him,
according to one account, the expedition's depleted money-chest.
He had been no friend of Hoffstetter, certainly.

'This semi-savage had not the slightest idea of discipline or
military order . . . His jackal eyes, his incomprehensible, jumbled,
half-Italian, half-Spanish tongue! All he could do was to ride ahead,
be the first to arrive at any camp, then throw himself full length on
the ground without attending to any of the needs of his men or
horses.'

157

Yet despite (or possibly because of?) his eccentricities Garibaldi had held him dear, even if he did exclaim on hearing the news, 'God be praised *he*'s gone.' Later, in his autobiography he was to write, 'One of the things most disagreeable to me during the Retreat was the desertion, especially of officers; and there were even some of my old companions in their number. Groups of them roamed through the country and committed outrages of every kind. Cowards in having abandoned the sacred cause of their country, it was natural that they should descend to obscene and cruel acts against their countrymen. This was what hurt me most of all . . . Some, caught in the act, were shot, but that was of little use, since most escaped scot free.'

The truth is that the army was now beginning to fade away. Again, it was not only the slaughter which was responsible. The defection of senior officers hardly set an encouraging example. The soldiers did not place the same confidence in those officers who were left. Then, pamphlets were widely distributed in St Angelo. The men did not enjoy seeing themselves described as monsters. All in all, discipline and morale were at a very low ebb – and never to rise again, either. It was at about this time, we are told by Ruggieri, that Garibaldi conceived the idea of leaving his disaffected men in the sanctuary of the Republic of San Marino, and attempting to reach Venice only with the faithful remnant.

One of our last dutiful acts before leaving St Angelo, and after saying goodbye to Professor Fini who had so kindly searched through the archives for us, was to visit the Duomo, next door to the commune, past the statue of the town's native Pope, Clement XIV.

There were many citizens, here as elsewhere, who defended the cause of their legitimate Sovereign, Pius IX; and who regarded, as he did, the preservation and handing-down of the Temporal Dominion – of St Peter's patrimony – as a sacred task. Their voice may now be heard – for Mgr Mengacci's sermon was among the papers we had just been given. I thumbed through it, as we sat on the steps:

'It was a wonderful spectacle for us to see thousands and thousands of liberating troops descend from the surrounding hills into the basin of the Metaurus; and to welcome here for the night the illustrious General, Count Stadion, with all his staff, and the Archduke Ernst and to see drawn up in our square a train of artillery . . .

Sant' Angelo in Vado (28-29 July)

'More wonderful still was the spectacle on August 4th when we welcomed the staff in full dress and many of the officers in our solemnly adorned cathedral church, to thank the Lord together with soldiers, united with each other, of many different tongues – Austrian, Bohemian, Hungarian, Polish, Croat . . . And to impart the Heavenly Benediction together with the Most High Sacrament . . . also to the crowds of people and troops who were not able to throng into our church, but paraded in the square . . . Who would not be moved by the sight of such splendour?'

XIX

Macerata Feltria

(29-30 July)

A WATERFALL, FORMED BY A SERIES of smooth, layered, slanting rocks, tumbled sonorously into a pool – almost a whirlpool – sending up a haze of spray on which the sun made rainbows, underneath a farmhouse perched high on the bank, and reached from a point opposite to our turning out of the main road, 1400 yards from St Angelo. This is one of the few impressive moments of the Metaurus which, like most of the rivers which come down from the Apennines into the Adriatic, runs for nearly all its course, after leaving the mountains proper, shallow and listless between a wilderness of untended banks. Here, at most seasons of the year, there is a roar and echo as the water plunges, and a sense of its power. To treat this as the prelude to our walk over to the next valley northwards was entirely proper, for it must have been either here or in the pools just above, that Garibaldi's horses had been watered that early morning of July 29th.

Our faces damp from the spray, we walked back past the hangar-like building of a new industrial estate, towards the farmstead of Carinalduccio. It seemed worthwhile to check the way from a girl, quite a pretty girl, who was getting out of a Fiat 500 by the church.

'Did you notice the very peculiar look that girl gave you?'

'No.'

'You realize you asked exactly the same girl the same question yesterday evening?'

'Ah, that would explain it.'

All the same, the country through which we were now to walk had been described by Hoffstetter as remote and desolate. There was that daunting phrase '*il gran nulla*'. Belluzzi talked of mountain paths that often got lost in the woods. And Trevelyan was even more forbiddingly lyrical, calling this 'one of the strangest regions in Italy: the higher mountains, naked peaks and tables, rear themselves on the skyline in fantastic fortress shapes, hard to distinguish, except by their size, from the works of man – the old robber castles perched on their summits. The aspect of the lesser hills, skeleton ridges washed bare of soil and corrugated by the rain torrents, baked by the sun into a hard white grey . . . is well-known in the backgrounds of Piero della Francesca etc. etc.' To double-check the way was a modest precaution.

But times have changed. A good gravel road led up through well-tilled arable land. True, one farm showed signs of wild neglect, roof-tiles missing, machinery rusting in the yard, clumps of nettles rampant in what once had been a garden. From its barn door an extraordinarily fat man emerged, carrying a bicycle across the threshold: mounting it, he freewheeled at great speed down the hills. Perhaps there is a correlation between extreme obesity and bad farming.

But beyond this, all the prospect was pleasing; for soon we came to a wide fold in which was set a serpentine lake bordered by poplars. Something which looked like a boat-house, but was probably a huntsman's hide, was concealed among the reeds at its furthest edge. Cattle browsed on the pale grass which swept down to its shores. At the head of the embracing valley we crossed a stone bridge, and looked down into the clear waters of a stream that fed it. And although the lake was clearly the creation of a resourceful farmer rather than of an eighteenth-century landscape gardener (for it was marked on none of our maps) the middle-distance view was nonetheless Arcadian, to the casual traveller. Had we been a little later, or a little warmer, we might have descended to its margin for a picnic.

On the far side of the stream our road slanted upwards. We passed beneath the well-laid dry-stone boundary wall of a farm built into the side of the hill, and commanding southern views not only of the delectable lake, but of layers of far-off hills, towards the black face of Monte Nerone and beyond. This was certainly a savager prospect. Then, at the crest of the rise, we looked northwards up to the grey spire of San Martino in Selvanera at the head of a larger, wooded valley, where the road ends; and, consulting our map, decided on a brave – well, *fairly* brave – detour along a path which must surely climb the highest ridge between us and the vale of the Foglia. It was sliced like a gash along the side of a bare hill; at the end of the track, in front of an abandoned farmhouse three huntsmen, green-gaitered, guns slung over their shoulders, whistled mechanically at their lean dogs. As we approached, they walked away slowly across the furrows of a field, not welcoming interruption.

'Rather an alarming little group.'

'They're timid Austrian scouts, that's all.'

'I see. You're Forbes, I suppose?'

Round about here, Forbes was putting up a very gallant rearguard show – if that is the right word for a Coldstreamer of that epoch. We now entered a deep trench, or cutting, rendered by the passage of tractors into a hideous yellow, squelchy quagmire. What a vile place for an ambush it would be! At its exit – and it seemed interminable – the path, just as Belluzzi had warned, lost itself in wood and scrub.

'We should have a guide, like *he* did. I told you so.'

'I shall simply have to steer by compass. We will wade on.'

The field was trackless, sodden. The prior of St Angelo had sought to excuse himself, when asked to explain why the city had let the Red Devil escape from the Austrian clutches, by cringing, 'A monster offered himself as a guide. The traitor, whose name is Costanzo Pasquini, is now far off.' We should not have minded a monster with us now.

Not that our loss of way was serious. Climbing up a hummock, by the side of one of those grey screes, or landslip-leftovers which scar many hillsides in these parts, we had our first vision of San Marino, the 'City of Refuge'. From far off its cliff-face seemed perpendicular, as unscaleable as a rock rising out of a stormy sea. Nearer to, lay or crouched the hulk of Monte Carpegna, that *massif* crowned by a colossal block which I suppose may have been a robber fortress but to me conjures up, rather, a megalithic barrow of some earth-god, some Titan: it is dark and the scale is inhuman.

Although we could not yet see down into the vale of the Foglia, the trickle, or rustle, of a streamlet on our left soon became louder. And, above the brambly ravine which it formed, a path was discovered that led steeply downhill, broadened – and plunged again to reach an area of neat allotments, this side of the broad riverbed of the Foglia. At last we arrived at the outskirts of the small town of Lunano. An enormous viaduct, of motorway dimensions, straddled the valley. We crossed it. Grass grew on its verges. Hens cackled on it. It started from nowhere, led to nowhere. Work was suspended. Beneath its great cement columns odd patches of some crop were planted.

'Do you think it was around here that Anita pleaded to be allowed to lead a foraging party, to collect maize for the horses?'

'You make it sound like a sentimental mission. Anyway, Garibaldi didn't let her.'

Certainly he did seize the opportunity, now that he was on level ground, to stop briefly and rest. During one of these halts, Hoffstetter says, the General 'harangued the soldiers before continuing the march, and was received more joyfully than ever. Here he shared with us his last cigar [singular] and a little fruit.'

From Lunano onwards the march did not grow any easier. Much of the time they stumbled along the dry, rocky bed of the river carved out by winter torrents.

We tried to follow dutifully in their footsteps. We pushed aside straggling copses of willows, plastic bags caught up in their branches: trod gingerly down piers of rubbish-dumps jutting out from the banks. In one shallow backwater the current eddied round the remains of an old boot.

'I feel rather like that suicide. In fact I shall *become* that suicide if we go on walking like this.'

'But I *enjoy* walking along riverbeds.'

Perhaps I should have shown more sympathy. The reference was to an unknown soldier, who had dropped out near here and was seen, as he sat on the bank of a ditch, to take off his shoes, point his rifle under his chin, and fire. On inspection both the dead man's feet were found to be hideously raw, hopelessly mangled. Evidently, not all the thousands of pairs of shoes, requisitioned in every city along the way, were enough to prevent such terrible lacerations, with which our own occasional footsoreness and blisters were, mercifully, not to be compared.

Until St Angelo, there had been few reports of casualties. But now death, as well as dissolution, was beginning to cast long shadows. In the steep-sided, poplar-wooded valley of the Apsa, on the road which leads up to Macerata Feltria, we paused to read an epigraph set into the wall of a wayside house:

Through these silent narrows
In 1849
Giuseppe Garibaldi
After the heroic defence of Rome
Passed with a few of his brave men
Pursued by foreign hordes
Whom here a Warrior taught
How to die, as the Spartans died,
Rather than to surrender
To tyrant invaders.

'But Garibaldi *didn't* die.'
'You can teach people how to face death, without dying yourself.'

I had already caught an echo of Greek history in the grove of the Sant'Angelo ambush. 'Between Metaurus and the mountain' had recalled 'Between Marathon and the sea'. But here was the first time we had encountered its deliberate evocation.

This march, a terrible twelve-hour stint, was especially exhausting for poor Anita (I should confess that we ourselves cheated in its latter half). When she arrived at Macerata in the evening she lay down at once on a small heap of straw, already afflicted by the first signs of the fever which was to kill her. A small, chipped stone monument, outside the city walls, marks the site of the shed where she took her brief rest; it had a roof but only two walls, for as a rule it was used to house a farm-cart. In an adjacent orchard the tent was hung between a cherry and an apple tree. There the General, in what seems a remarkably good mood for the circumstances ('ottima luna'), ate roast chicken with his staff. Wine, water and two barrels of cod were also brought by the citizens to the troops. All around, camp fires blazed, and Garibaldi was happy to see this, too; for he intended to change camp in a few hours, and the fires would serve to deceive his pursuers. Towards ten forty-five that same night marching orders were given to the commanders of the two legions, Forbes and Sacchi.

There was, however, some difficulty in persuading his men to move. It is impossible not to sympathize with them. The General went so far as to fire some shots in the air, hoping that the false alarm would help in assembling his men. Patrols were sent into the town to root them out from the cafés: some of them used their sabres too freely. Insults were exchanged involving senior officers, who found themselves reduced to the ranks.

The importance of military discipline is emphasized more than ever by Hoffstetter, in these later stages when everything around him was collapsing. He devotes several paragraphs to deploring the inexperience of too many of the volunteers whose first taste of war had been during the Defence of Rome and the Retreat; and who still did not know how to address superiors properly, and touchily took reprimands as personal affronts. The disorderly call to arms at Macerata, and the shambles that followed, offended his sense of propriety more than anything that had happened so far. It was thoroughly *disagreeable*.

They even left, it may be, some of their muskets behind them. For, in one corner of the commune archives, behind a step-ladder, behind dusty rolls and parchments, a small cache was stacked, and produced for our inspection. Everyone in the Commune was splendidly helpful, but since none of us, not even the attendant policeman, could claim to have any knowledge of historic firearms we could neither affirm nor deny the local tradition that these three or four percussion rifles had, indeed, belonged to the Garibaldini of the day. A small crown stamped on their butts appeared to testify to their imperial Austrian origin; but this would by no means preclude their having come into the hands of the legionaries.

'Pictures must be taken. Point a gun out of the window, down into the square. Try to look more *soldierly*.'

'I think I would have dropped out long before this. Or anyway been one of the ones who left their guns behind.'

Other memorabilia were kindly laid out before us: an oleograph of the period showing the General standing before a tumbledown hut, with three or four of his officers – looking, for once, more gloomy than heroic: and a thick file of municipal records of 1849. Most of the topical papers related to payments demanded by carters who had been impressed and trekked long miles in the service either of Garibaldi or of the Austrians who were to enter the city shortly after he had left. In both cases, of course, it was the Commune who eventually had to bear the cost, considerable correspondence ensuing in efforts to recover at least a portion from neighbouring towns.

Our own departure was made in good order, indeed with ceremony; for we were escorted through the town to observe the statue of the General (one of the very few which, appropriately, represent him as a forty-year-old officer rather than as a veteran Saviour) and to admire the cathedral, in which, as usual, a solemn Te Deum was celebrated after the troubles were over.

XX

On the Road to San Marino

(30-31 July)

THE RELEVANT SHEET of the Military Geographical Institute, if anyone else should ever wish to follow the tracks of Garibaldi's last stage from Macerata to San Marino, is 108. Belluzzi, many decades later, went over it in ten hours on a donkey, and wrote, 'I think an exact itinerary can't be shown because the Garibaldini, tired, harassed, devoured by hunger and thirst, found it only too easy to scatter, hoping to find, as they got away and gathered together in isolated huts or hovels, an odd hour's rest, a scrap of cloth to rebandage their feet, a drop of water and a crust of bread . . .'

Given the dissolution of this ragged band, it does great credit to Garibaldi's reputation that the Austrians should still consider him so dangerous, and treat him so warily. Field-Marshal D'Aspre writes in his account of the Retreat '. . . on the 30th of July, near Carpegna, Garibaldi made an attempt to break out once again into Tuscany, but three companies of Stadion's brigade, coming from Pennabilli, frustrated this attempt.'

Not that this was an option which the General had altogether discarded when in Macerata. During his brief stay he asked questions about mountain routes back westward – not indeed into Tuscany but towards Castrocaro, and thence down to Forlì in the Romagna. Arduous way to reach the sea, and Venice!

I should be very happy to go over this ground again, and try to establish beyond doubt precisely where the engagement – or near-engagement – took place. That it was near Carpegna seems certain. But where is the foot of the high cliff? Hoffstetter's paragraph is worth quoting, for this was the last time any semblance of order was imposed: and that in itself seems a most extraordinary achievement, after so many days and nights of marching, such heat, deluges, sleeplessness, fatigue, footsoreness, desertion. After twelve hours'

167

marching on the previous day they left Macerata late at night, and arrived at a monastery at the foot of a cliff 'fashioned like an unscaleable wall' towards midday on July 30th.

'At four in the afternoon the advance posts spied the enemy's vanguard, who soon arrived in full sight of us, at the distance of a cannon-shot. The General immediately made dispositions: one cohort stayed in occupation of the cloisters, two companies were placed one hundred yards behind on the right, on a small shoulder of the rock; and another two on the left, in and behind a few small houses. The rest of the infantry was drawn up in two lines above a meadow which sloped gently down towards the enemy, with the cannon positioned on the left; the troop was on the left of, and at the same height as, the monastery. Behind this wing we drew up the cavalry, and the baggage train was above a little road which leads to Pennabilli in the valley of the Conca (*sic*). As the enemy showed no more signs of activity, the General ordered the column to move by the left, while a violent storm drenched us. He rode at the head of the cavalry and the baggage train, then followed the cohorts of the left wing, then the garrison of the cloisters; and bringing up the rear, the troops which were behind the cloisters . . . Night had already fallen when we crossed the re-entrant of the valley of the Conca . . . at eleven o'clock we entered a large wood . . . the baggage train had taken a wrong turning, from which I rescued it at midnight . . . I found some hay for the horses in an isolated farm, but couldn't find any food or water at all.'

We ourselves explored the site of the convent of Pietrarubbia, suggested by Ruggieri, Belluzzi and Trevelyan. It didn't seem to fit.

'No *very high* cliff.'

'If only there was still a monastery here, we could ask them about that woollen blanket which the fathers were said to have shown visitors – which Garibaldi took a nap on.'

'*Altissima rupe* must refer to a face of Carpegna.'

It was reminiscent of the search for the narrow, wooded defile after Orvieto. The temptation, implausibly, to blame giant bulldozers for restructuring of the landscape crept over us.

At last we left Mercato Vecchio, turning right at the hopefully-named Cappuccini crossroads, still searching and guessing. Somewhere near here Belluzzi reports a particularly gory incident, typical of the minor hideousness of war. Six Garibaldini who had gone to ground were discovered and pulled out by a squad of

Austrian soldiers from their hiding place into the middle of the
road, and shot. One of them, riddled with bullets, dragged himself
as far as a cattle-stall, where he tried to staunch his bleeding with
handfuls of straw. He lived, twitching and screaming, until dawn
and no one dared to come to his aid in the general terror. The
corpses of all six were burnt with lime, and the priest refused them
burial in the local cemetery.

'Let us put that queasy story behind us, before having our lunch.'
'Very heartless of you.'

But four kilometres on we came to an imposing bridge over a
deep ravine which the River Conca, already at this short distance
from its source, has carved out. By this time, search for the lost
monastery had produced an appetite which – false to pretend
otherwise – no legend of Austrian brutality could spoil.

Above and to the west of us, the waters tumbled between sheer
rock-faces, forming a series of jewelled waterfalls. Carrying our
picnic away from the road, we followed a path, made soft underfoot
by pine-needles, which agreeably up-and-downed over heathery
hummocks and stone outcrops, until arriving at the foot of a fall,
whose splashing, greeny-white waters had scooped out whorls in
the rocks, as though to echo and justify the name of the river –
Conca or shell.

'I should like to eat my picnic just a little higher where it's not so
noisy, and you can still hear the nightingales.'
'No. I want to see the fish in the pools. If there are any.'

The rival merits of fish and birds were surprisingly hard to
resolve. For several minutes we carried our supplies alternately
nearer to, and further from, the water, the site of the picnic
becoming even more contentious than the site of the monastery.

An invasion by an army of ants succeeded an uneasy
compromise, as we sat on a bank, by the roots of a pine tree, and cut
our bread and salami.

'Look at them. Totally ridiculous animals, lugging that rind to
and fro. Why on earth don't they keep still, and just eat it?'
'A giant ant watching us might say the same.'

Sun, shining between the branches of the pine trees and wine
restored harmony and, to quote Belluzzi who stopped near here
during his journey on donkey-back, we enjoyed '*un' ora di riposo
dolcissimo*'.

It was, we reckoned, very near here, on the night of July 30-31st, after their retreat from the monastery near Carpegna, that the remnants of the army enjoyed not very much more than one hour of what must have been far sweeter – or at least far more needed – repose. For if they had entered the large wood at eleven o'clock, and placed a few pickets around the glade where they lay to rest, it was less than two hours later that they resumed their march at one o'clock in the morning. Hoffstetter rhapsodizes over their departure, '. . . in the most splendid moonlight and utter silence. Without a word spoken we first passed through several meadows, then took the direct road towards San Marino, up a narrow valley, from which we emerged at sunrise, finding ourselves on the eastern slope of the Apennines. Magnificent view! Beneath us, there extended a vast plain, and beyond that the sea in all its majesty. Like proud swans, the boats gilded by the sun ploughed the surface smooth as a mirror while the waves, touched with azure, saluted in friendship the coast of emerald, on which how pleasantly were strewn the cities of Cesenatico, Rimini and Pesaro! . . . The mountain here, steep and rocky, hems the prosperous plain that extends northwards to Bologna and Ravenna, further than the eye can see; and southwards to the point where the Abruzzi come down to the shore . . . The lowland country stretches out magnificent, green as the sea is blue, criss-crossed by fine roads, covered by great cities, furrowed by the Metaurus and the Rubicon and the many torrents that mingle their crystalline waters with the Adriatic. Everyone's gaze roamed with longing over the saviour sea towards one goal, and in our mind's eye we saw rise out of that blue horizon our last star, our last hope, the City of the Lagoons!

'On the plain between the mountain and Rimini, there rises, perpendicular, one enormous rock. This is the territory of the Republic of San Marino. The city itself covers only a small part of the surface of the rock . . . whose summit is crowned by two ancient castles. To our right and to our left ranged the Apennines, at midnight looking so rocky and bare, at midday green and clothed by ancient ruins and beautiful, small hill-cities. Everyone, officers and soldiers, moved forwards and gazed in wonder at this magnificent picture.

'Hereabouts the General halted the rearguard. He directed the column, now only one thousand eight hundred men strong, into the narrow valley which was all that now divided us from the rock of the Republic. The cavalry was ordered to climb to the opposite side of the valley – minor trespass, forced by tactics, upon the neutral territory. Together with a small escort he hurried towards the city, following the high contour.'

The distant prospect, which we surveyed from the saddle between Monte Copiolo and Monte San Marco, is still much as Hoffstetter described. The blue waves now give their friendly salute to a line of skyscraper hotels – children's toy blocks seen from this height. The sun now gilds a tanker or two, and a natural-gas rig, on the horizon. The cities are certainly larger, the roads (it might be argued) even more beautiful. But the vast bowl which lay at our feet is almost as sparsely inhabited and as wild as in his day.

We decided that, for our own final walk, we would make a circuit of this whole terrain, a loop walk starting and finishing at San Marino: we would follow the contour along which the General cantered, discover where the precious cannon, dragged all the way from Rome with no shot fired, was toppled to its resting place, and imagine (if not locate) the spot where Anita brandished her whip in an attempt to rally the faltering, confused Garibaldini at the foot of the rock.

'All over the ground we're looking at patrols were departing and *not* returning. There were twos and threes, scattered everywhere.'

'As ragged as us.'

We gazed north-east, to that other abrupt rock-city of St Leo, on towards Verucchio. From here one patrol *had* returned, to report that Austrians were arriving from the north – from Bologna.

The encirclement of the Garibaldini was complete.

✤XXI✤
San Marino
(31 July–1 August)

O N THE FOLLOWING MORNING, then, the trinketry of the
streets of San Marino well behind us, we crossed the border of
the Republic, back into Italy, just before reaching the tiny village of
Monte. The surfaced road ends here, and there is a choice of many
tracks. The one we chose led past a domain screened by a box-hedge
fragrant after rain – a dark and secret tunnel of a path until, after a
few yards, it plunged precipitously down to the white-stoned bed of
the Mazzocco. This is an uninviting *torrente*, unshaded, a place for
snakes. And the track upwards on the other side of the bridge was
inhospitable, too, savage even, long root-tendrils of broom clinging
tenaciously to the steep and shaly banks between which we walked.

Looking straight ahead, the shoulder of wooded Monte Copiolo,
where we had stood the day before, seemed impossibly distant in
the shimmery haze of the morning. To the east, on the other side of
the bowl, the whale-back of Monte San Paolo, down whose flanks
the Austrians had crowded to fire upon the Garibaldini, promised
us an easier walk – the loop of our return.

In one farmyard a shawled woman, summoned by the barking of
her dogs, and carrying a pail of food for her hens, came out from a
barn to see who we were.

'*English?*' she repeated after me, then pointed back to the village
of Monte. It was not so much a question, more an instruction, curt
dismissal even. Perhaps we had not made ourselves altogether clear.
Should I attempt my standard Garibaldi apologia – but it seemed
unlikely that she would be very interested. Nor was I sure that I
could spare the time. One of the dogs was snarling, raising its top lip
to bare yellow teeth.

'We are walking to Campo d'Arco, up and around the top of the
valley.'

'The wrong way,' she insisted. 'You are taking the wrong way for the Englishman. He has been here for many years. The son has been wounded.'

She pointed again.

'But . . .' For an insane moment I thought – could she be referring to the Englishman Forbes or his son or a descendant of some sort or other? Forbes had certainly helped Anita rally the troops beneath Monte San Paolo. '. . . we are on foot' I ended lamely.

'There is no point in walking up there, none at all,' she repeated, and walked, rather crossly, back into the barn. Her dogs followed her.

The mystery of the Englishman remained with us, not to be solved until later in the evening.

Meanwhile, we climbed up to the cluster of houses called Pugliano, nestling in a fold of the hill: then took a path, more or less along the contour, towards the chapel at the head of the valley. There had been other Campo d'Arco's on our journey, other evocatively named 'fields of the bow'; and re-entrants of many valleys I suppose may fairly thus be described – their curvature, as you climb towards them, not unlike that of a bow drawn taut.

From this chapel, the halfway point of our walk – the top of the loop, as it were – all the paths, save the one we had come up, burrowed into the great wood, in some corner or glade of which Garibaldi had briefly rested before his disorderly march to the borders of the Republic.

'*I* think that was much nearer the picnic of the Great Ant.'

Another problem unsolved. Impossible to locate exactly where, in the forests that clothe Monte Copiolo, his army, part of it losing their way, stumbled that night. What is certain is that dawn saw him riding along the high slopes of Monte San Paolo, and it was this course we followed as soon as we emerged from the woodland paths. For us, an idyll of a walk; because it is hard to exaggerate the pleasure, ecstasy even, of ambling through sunlit, upland meadows, dotted blue with gentian, the noise of bird-song all around, a hare occasionally bounding. Ascents and descents were leisurely. At one corner of the track, we rested on a bank, in the shade of an oak; and took a compass bearing on the ancient castles of San Marino, and on the rock of San Leo; and found ourselves back within a mile of Monte. As though to reward us for successful navigation (not, it is true, very difficult in this terrain) a gurgle at the side of the path came to our ears. An odd, but agreeable noise. There, framed in a plot of grass, was a tiny pool, no larger than a foot in diameter, which gushed in a rhythm too irregular to be called a heartbeat. Now every second, now a pause of two or three seconds, and the crystal water of the spring bubbled up, formed a crown, and subsided. In the crystal waters of this miniature fountain we bathed our faces.

A few yards further on, the ground to our right fell away steeply and we looked down into a rocky hollow – or funnel might be a better word, so steep were its sides. Here, surely, was the correct place to re-enact in our imagination the demise of that cannon which, for so many weary miles, had been dragged along by mules, by oxen – and occasionally even borne on the shoulders of its guardians.

It was seven or eight o'clock in the morning of July 31st. Garibaldi himself had gone ahead to San Marino to treat with the Captain-Regent. The main body was negotiating a deep hollow. Some men were on the near lip, some at the bottom, and some climbing the far side. Halfway down, the cannon, jolting along a particularly rough piece of ground, struck a rock, broke or fractured its rudder, and all but crashed out of control to the bottom of the precipice.

Everybody halted. Time was needed to make some rough and ready repairs. Exhausted, hungry, dripping with sweat and with blood, their feet lacerated, the men needed no better excuse for falling out. They lay down and for two hours took what rest they could. The rearguard, pickets and scouts gradually rejoined the men on the near side of the hollow, mingled with them, and added to the confusion. No better formula for disaster can be imagined.

The Austrians, told of their opportunity by spies, concentrated a force on Monte San Paolo – along whose contours we had just walked – and descended 'with the ferocity of a pack of wolves thirsting for blood'. Rockets were fired down into the hollow. There was panic. No attempt was made to form a rearguard, or to turn and fight. The cannon was abandoned, the Austrians blocked it and shoved it contemptuously to the bottom of the cliff.

(Later, they were to force their prisoners, two of them wounded, to haul it to Archduke Ernst's headquarters at Fiorentino, just beneath the city.)

In San Marino itself, the noise and echoes of the firing could be heard, and the white coats of the Austrians clearly seen descending

Monte San Paolo. The General and his staff hurried back to the scene of the action and found Anita (brandishing a whip and red with rage) and Forbes the only two who were attempting to stay the rout. But the enemy did not press their pursuit, and at last the Garibaldini scrambled, more or less in one body, up the far side of the hollow, to relative safety.

They pitched their camp immediately outside the walls of the city. However, Garibaldi was now so disgusted by the conduct of his men that he told Hoffstetter he could do no more with such a horde: his only course was to disband them. Hoffstetter did not attempt to dissuade him. What could be done with troops who did not stand up to fire? With men most of whom no longer had shoes, whose officers were fed up with a campaign that offered no hope, whose horses and mules were either ungovernable or almost dead with fatigue? Much better to negotiate that they should be able to return to their own homes rather than they should fall into prison. The General would in every way be better off without soldiers whom, should there be a battle, he could neither trust nor, with honour, abandon.

Negotiations! The Captain-Regent of San Marino, Belzoppi, conducted them throughout with great skill. They could be said to have been initiated when, at one o'clock two mornings earlier an envoy of Garibaldi, galloping from Macerata, arrived in the Republic. Ever since the bloodthirsty affair at Sant'Angelo odd groups of armed deserters, on horseback, had been turning up to the growing alarm of the citizens. But now the red-shirted Francesco Nullo, the General's quartermaster, accompanied by twelve lancers, came to ask that formal permission be granted for the passage of the army through the neutral territory of San Marino.

Nullo deserves a footnote. He was the most dashing and personable of the young officers, a future hero of the Sicilian expedition and the capture of Palermo in 1860. Later still he was to give his life for the cause of the liberation of Poland. He was described as casual, extravagant, proud, aquiline – 'the sort of officer that Napoleon would have made a Colonel of Dragoons, and thrown with his regiment, on horseback, into the breach of a city under bombardment'.

With great tact Belzoppi explained to the young Nullo that the General's arrival in San Marino would cause a most critical situation and, without being of any furtherance to his own cause, would gravely compromise the safety of the Republic, powerless as it was. He appealed to his principles which would lead him to wish to conserve 'this ancient asylum of peace and liberty'. His letter to the General is a masterpiece of dissuasion.

'The nearby shore cannot afford you means of embarkation, since for some days all the boats have been keeping well out to sea; the concentration of Austrian troops has grown greatly over the last two days; a general is at their head and they have been joined by cavalry; yesterday, what is more, they sent pickets of observers towards the borders of our Republic.'

After this it may come as an anti-climax to learn that Nullo lost his way back to his General, or at least was unable to cross through the Austrian lines. Late next evening Belzoppi had to deal with an even more pressing and formal delegation. This was headed by Ugo Bassi, who delivered into his hands a letter of intent demanding provisions and passage at once. Their exchange (which has a Thucydidean ring) is recorded as follows by the military adviser of the Republic, Oreste Brizi, writing in 1850:

Belz: 'The Government of the Republic cannot grant armed passage through its territory to the Garibaldi band, because reasons of external and internal policy forbid it.'
Bassi: 'I did not expect such a reply from the representative of a republic, and hoped for greater sympathy for our cause from the Government of San Marino.'
Belz: 'But how do you mean to reconcile sympathies or antipathies with the neutrality that our situation imposes upon us, and thanks to which we have been and shall be as we are? Heaven forbid we abandon it!'
Bassi: 'And if Garibaldi comes, what will you do?'
Belz: 'We shall protest. For a state which has no arms to make its rights respected, words are all that is left to oppose force.'
Bassi: 'But the army is starving, has need of provisions, and cannot procure them from any but you.'
Belz: 'Here humanity can play its part, and if Garibaldi's army is hungry, we will supply provisions tomorrow, at our borders, which must not be crossed. Only in this way can matters be settled. Do you accept?'
Bassi: 'I do, if that is what my General wishes.'

A messenger now had to be sent back to the General with the terms. The night ride must have been terrifying. Austrian camp fires blazed all around. Ugo Bassi watched them with dismay, from an inn in the Republic.

It was to accept these conditions that next morning at nine o'clock Garibaldi and his staff arrived in the principal street of San Marino, and without dismounting proceeded at once to the government palace. By this time his men, after their rout in the hollow, had already trespassed over the borders of the Republic. For this, he made a passing apology:

'Citizen Regent! Pursued by overwhelming Austrian forces, my troops, broken by hardships of every sort suffered in mountains and in the wilds, are no longer fit to fight, and it was necessary to cross your borders for a few hours' rest and for bread. They will lay down their arms in your Republic, where the Roman war for the independence of Italy now ceases. I come amongst you as a refugee: accept me as such, and let no ill come to you with the Austrian, through your saving of me and of those who have followed me.'

The Captain-Regent did not refer in his reply to any displeasure or alarm he may have felt at the unwelcome invasion. He instantly seized the most important word in Garibaldi's address:

'Welcome to the refugee. This hospitable land receives you, General. Rations for your soldiers are being prepared, your wounded are being taken in and cared for. The exchange you owe is to spare this land from the evils and disasters we fear. I accept the mandate of mediation which you offer me: that service is another humanitarian office which I am glad to render you.'

After promising that during his brief stay in the Republic he would not attack the Austrians if they did not first attack him, Garibaldi established a headquarters at the monastery of the Capuchins. He was told that one officer, consigning a wounded man to their care, had said '*Quod uni ex minimis meis fecistis, mihi fecistis*'; and he expressed surprise that any of his officers should be able to quote the gospels – forgetting (I can only suppose) that Ugo Bassi was in the uniform of an officer rather than of a priest.

As he sat speaking to the brothers, a soldier came up and begged him for shoes. He pointed to his own pair, the worn-out soles of which flapped open, and offered an exchange.

Using a drum as a table-top, he wrote his final proclamation to his men. 'We are arrived in this land of refuge, and we owe our best behaviour to our generous hosts, if we are to deserve the consideration due to our misfortunes. From this hour I release my companions-in-arms from all obligations whatsoever, leaving them free to return to private life. But I remind them that they must not remain in a state of disgrace, and that it is better to die than to live as slaves of the foreigner.'

There was now little he could do, save to visit his wounded and to comfort Anita, until he learnt the result of the negotiations set on foot by the Captain-Regent. The first reply was not encouraging. Archduke Ernst, who had pursued Garibaldi from Sant'Angelo and was now camped with his 2500 exhausted men at Fiorentino just underneath the city, took out a pencil and scribbled that his terms were unconditional surrender: acting in the name of the Pope, against the enemies of the legitimate government, he would accept no less.

This news found the General by the side of Anita, who was lying on the floor, in a bundle of rags, in the house of Simoncini. In a white rage, he put his uniform back on, and went out among his men, trying to rally them. Anita accompanied him. Many – perhaps most – of his soldiers and men were either snatching a rest or eating. He was heard shouting at them, 'The Italian is a good soldier but he likes to eat four hours a day and sleep sixteen.'

This does sound rather hard on men who had been either marching or fighting, since one o'clock that morning. Perhaps the rest by the side of the cannon, and the rout, was still rankling him.

The outcome of his fiery incitations was that the envoy returned, in alarm, to plead once more with the Archduke. The size of the Republic's army was emphasized, no more than a hundred men at the most. It would be impossible to prevent Garibaldi from seizing all the strongpoints in the city, should he choose. Archduke Ernst, who was resting from the heat under the shade of a great elm tree and possibly had little taste for immediate combat, relented and assured the envoy that for the time being at least, he would not open fire unless he was attacked first.

Nerves remained taut. There were false alarms, and sporadic shots.

A second embassy had been sent to General de Hahne at Rimini, the Archduke's superior officer. Towards evening the envoys returned, bringing much more favourable terms. Here is a précis:

1. Arms to be laid down and handed over to the Austrian command.
2. Army to be disbanded. Men to be organized in units according to their provinces they belonged to, and escorted home. Safe conduct except for those convicted of common crime.
3. Republic of San Marino to receive compensation in horses and equipment.
4. Troops to remain in the Republic until the terms have been signed by the Commander-in-Chief, Gorzkowski.
5. Austrians meanwhile not to attack.
6. Garibaldi and his wife to receive passports and go to America.
7. Truce to be guaranteed by two representatives of the Republic and two senior officers of Garibaldi going to the Rimini head-quarters and remaining as hostages until the terms were signed.

The San Marino envoy had prudently managed to water down the original demand that Garibaldi should '. . . be *exiled for ever* to America'.

Even so, the terms could scarcely be expected to be to the General's liking. He received them from the hands of the Captain-Regent in the government palace, and immediately summoned his senior officers to confer with him in Simoncini's house. Here he read the articles out to the silent, grim circle.

We, too, had before us a copy of them, extracted from Folio 169 of the Republic's archives; and we sat and read them as, our long walk over, we rested in what is now the café Garibaldi. The plaque on the wall was inscribed:

> In this room
> On the 31st July 1849
> Giuseppe Garibaldi
> Having heard from the mediators
> Of the Republic of San Marino
> The terms of the surrender imposed upon him
> Uttered the Spartan words
> A REPUBLICAN NEVER SURRENDERS
> And, having rejected the humiliating message
> Of the enemy invaders
> Consecrated his name to immortality

'I'm not sure it was *quite* like that.'

'I don't know. He was furious about being asked for *hostages*. Also he didn't like the exclusion from the amnesty of soldiers convicted of common crimes.'

'I suppose too many of his men *had* been.'

A burly young man hovered over us. Was he eavesdropping? Perhaps it was unfair to be suspicious. It is not uncommon to be stared at in Italian cafés, nor is it a sign of ill manners. We may have been looking even odder, certainly more tattered than when we had set out from Rome. Stout walking-boots are not often seen in the streets of this town of tourism and philately, summer clothes the general rule of visitors up from the coast. The man was probably trying to decide what foreign language we were speaking. German? That his face was scarred, and one of his arms in plaster, in a sling, did not necessarily mean that he was dangerous, or had been involved in some brawl. On the contrary, it could be said to render him more harmless. Objection could not seriously be taken. However, as the minutes passed, a mild temptation grew to cast him as one of those desperate members of the General's band whose behaviour grew worse and worse as discipline dissolved.

'That man who nearly killed a fellow-soldier in some fight? His colonel – Forbes I expect – wanted to shoot him out of hand for *disturbing the good order and tranquillity of the Republic.*'

'A good touch. Who had disturbed it in the first place?'

'Or he might be the chap who tried to stab the sleeping officer, to pinch his money-belt. He looks like that. Used to a life of crime.'

Our conversation drifted to the local criminals of those days: for example, it was said that the worst profiteers, who bought up the Garibaldini's arms and horses at rock-bottom prices, were those of San Marino's extreme left, the 'ultra-democratic' party, exactly the people who *should* have supported Garibaldi's cause. 'Long live Red Fraternity' Brizi comments, sourly.

The young man continued to inspect us. At last he put his uninjured arm on the back of my chair, leaned over and said,

'New Maldon.'

'I beg your pardon?'

'I thought I heard you talking about New Maldon. Mind if I sit down? I come from near there. What are you drinking?'

What awful things might he have overheard us saying? Hadn't we accused him of theft, murder, rape possibly? The mystery of

New Maldon could wait. He sounded unaggressive – amiable even, for one who had been accused of such a catalogue of century-old crimes. All the same there were one or two guns hung criss-cross on the wall: I seem to remember a sabre as well. It seemed prudent to establish a historical context for what we had been saying, make it clear that our accusations were purely fanciful, in no way reflected on him personally.

I said, 'Actually, we were talking about Garibaldi. You know, Garibaldi.'

'These Italian politicians – they're all the same.'

'But this café is called after him.'

'You can't tell anything from that. Doesn't make a blind bit of difference.'

His last remark was, of course, perfectly true – could even be said to be a premise from which we had started from Rome. Nobody thinks of St James in St James's. But here, *here* in this eponymous café where no fewer than three plaques commemorated the Hero – one outside, one on the wall of the room in which we were sitting, one upstairs where poor Anita had uneasily slept? This was testing Max Beerbohm's theory to destruction.

'What was it you said about New Maldon?' Since he was clearly uninterested in Garibaldi I would spare him my standard lecture.

'No, no. It was you that said something about New Maldon. Something about guards I thought I heard. Couldn't quite catch. I'm a guard myself, you see. Inner Circle. Nice to hear English spoken again. Been cooped up here for months.' He smacked his plaster.

He talked, then, of keeping order at certain tube stations late at night, a task which would have taxed any of Garibaldi's officers. It would have taxed even Anita, with her whip. Things in the early morning were much more peaceful. It was possible to stop at some stations – I have forgotten which – for quite leisurely cups of tea.

'You get to know the ones which do the best tea.'

'Don't the passengers get impatient?'

'Got the power of life and death over them, I have. A guard can do anything. He's in charge.'

A suitable attitude, I suppose, for a ferryman – a Charon – of the underworld to express. Then it struck me that a mumbled 'New Maldon' might well sound very like a mumbled 'Garibaldi', especially as out of habit I may have used the English pronunciation of the General's name. Another connection suggested itself. Might this possibly be the wounded Englishman of whom the woman in the farmyard, on the foothills of Monte Copiolo, had spoken?

And indeed it was. His Italian grandparents had told him something about Garibaldi – he couldn't remember what – during the long summer holidays he had spent at their home near Monte as a boy. There was, he thought, a statue of the old chap further up in the town. And he knew all the paths from San Marino towards Longiano, down over the wide riverbed of the Marecchia, along one of which Garibaldi, with the last faithful two hundred of his followers, escaped on the night of July 31st.

For the General had, in the end, scribbled a brief note to the Captain-Regent, 'The conditions imposed on us by the Austrians are unacceptable, and therefore we will unburden your land – Yours G. Garibaldi.'

It was in this same room that our own walk could be said to close, our way and the General's to part. For us, return to the land of the Inner Circle was uneventful. Let Hoffstetter, then, true Xenophon of the long march, our unfailing companion all the way from Rome, close the tale. His account begins with the summoning of the staff to the house of Simoncini, to hear the 'unacceptable terms'.

'Solemn, silent, we stood round our beloved condottiere, who explained to us, succinctly, that he was forced to disband his men, and that thanks to the generous assistance of the government of San Marino he had successfully concluded an armistice with the Austrians, and an agreement which would afford protection to all his companions-in-arms – but that this was dependent on ratification by the Commander-in-Chief, which could not arrive from Bologna before noon on the following day. I then spoke and tried to show we could presume that it was the Austrian intention to take the General prisoner, alone; and that possibly by midday tomorrow San Marino, which was at present threatened from the south and the east, would be surrounded on its other side as well. Then, perhaps, ratification would not be forthcoming, and we should be forced to accept quite different terms. Therefore the General should not wait for the moment when the ratification fell due. It was our duty to persuade him to leave that very night. He should not sign the conditions, but keep the treaty with him until the last possible moment before his departure, and then send it back with a note of rejection. So far as the men were concerned, there was on the whole nothing to fear. Or else we could arrange for the treaty to be signed by the senior officer who stayed behind – because only a few wished to follow the General further – who could then return it with a clause saying that Garibaldi had left the command in his hands, and gone. We should inform all sections of the army of our decision so that those who felt themselves too gravely compromised could still join the General, despite the danger they would face.

'Most of those present declared themselves in agreement, and the General gave me a special word of thanks.

'His wife had been taken very ill the previous day, and wasn't able to leave her bed – very understandable in her condition. But no one, least of all her anxious and faithful husband, foresaw the sad conclusion . . .

'At nightfall we mounted horse, and rode down to the lower town, leaving by the Rimini gate. A brief halt at the foot of the mountain to wait for those who might wish to leave with us. The General with his wife (who was scarcely able to keep in the saddle), and Ciceruacchio rode ahead with a guide for several miles, dismounting in a coppice by the side of the road . . . Bit by bit we were joined by about two hundred men (including one hundred horse), mostly officers. I stayed behind here for a whole hour, expecting many others to come too . . . at last, my wait seemed too long. It was a clear moonlit night. The snorting and whinnying of the horses could betray us to the enemy . . . so I left and soon came up to the General. He shook his head in sorrow, when I told him that none of his other officers were following. There had been about two–three hundred crowns left over in the war-chest from yesterday's pay-day, and these had disappeared too; so that the General who never carried a penny on his own person, was to find himself, when at last he arrived at Genoa, without any means of support whatsoever . . .'

Sad contrast to the brave departure from Rome! Who else would have been so foolish as to continue, even, to hope?

EPILOGUE

WHAT HAPPENED to everyone afterwards?

Hoffstetter, poor fellow, got lost just after crossing the Rubicon, a few miles further on. He found himself alone with his servant. He had no map. All he knew was that enemy patrols were all around. He knocked at several doors, asking to be let in, in order to change out of his uniform into the civilian clothes which, with extraordinary foresight, he had managed to keep with him; and was distressed to find how different his reception was, now that he had no men with him. People said they would be shot if they opened their doors to an officer of Garibaldi. To raise money he had to sell his horses, and to accept the pitiful sum of twenty-five crowns for all three of them. And, he says, that included the fine English saddles and bridles! He made sure they were fed first, then saw them go with tears in his eyes. He buried his sword, with its fine Toledo blade, his 'beautiful' dagger, and his pair of captured French pistols, hoping one day to come back and find them. Then he made his way through Lombardy to his home in Switzerland, by means of a network of sympathizers. There he passes out of history; I have been able to discover nothing more about him whatsoever.

*　　*　　*

The bulk of the army, finding themselves abandoned in San Marino, at first panicked and then threatened to continue the fight. Calmed down by the remaining officers, they eventually laid down their arms at the gate of San Francesco, and left the Republic in twos and threes, wearing clothes expensively purchased through the sale of their arms and horses. Along the way the Austrians arrested them, beat some of them up, and escorted them to Rimini.

Here they were treated according to the 'unacceptable' terms – even although these had been neither signed by Garibaldi, nor ratified by Gorzkowski. That is to say, all those not convicted of crimes were duly permitted to return to their home provinces.

About fifty men, however, hid in San Marino, and later declared that they did not wish to return home, but preferred exile. For these, the San Marino government negotiated a free passage through Tuscany to Genoa. What magnanimous treatment, Brizi says, of the remnants of that armed band which last month had disturbed the peace of the Grand Duchy! Had sought to raise a revolution, incite new vendettas, bring new misfortunes; had arrested and dragged with them peaceful religious, respectable ecclesiastics, and a worthy Government functionary . . . !

*   *   *

Citizen Colonel Forbes erected street barricades against the Austrians, on Garibaldi's arrival at the small port of Cesenatico on August 1st; and was the last to embark on one of the fishing boats of the tiny, commandeered fleet that was to sail up the Adriatic, making for Venice. His boat was captured by the Austrian brig *Oreste*, and he was imprisoned in Pola, to be released in October through the good offices of the British representative and the Foreign Office. During the 'fifties he went to America, became a fencing-master, and a hanger-on of the *New York Tribune*. John Brown offered him a job at 100 dollars a month to teach his soldiers drill in Iowa, but there was violent dispute over money (in which Forbes was clearly in the wrong). He threatened to expose Brown's plans to Republican Senators, and in the end did so. He wrote begging-letters saying, 'If my family were from any circumstances to be in distress, that distress ought cheerfully and effectually to be alleviated by anti-slavery men of every school.'

More happily, he was to take some part in the Sicilian campaign in 1860, suggesting to Garibaldi that he should raise a British Legion. Again there were difficulties over money, although the banker Henry Hoare contributed £750. He died in poverty in Pisa. I have failed to discover what happened to his young son, left behind in San Marino. Attempting to trace subsequent Forbes connections in Italy, I came across the record of a James Forbes who 'died of apoplexy while dancing in Florence', and like to think that this spirited member of the family may have been a descendant.

*　　*　　*

Father Ugo Bassi was all but left behind in San Marino; he was not in Simoncini's house, and did not hear of Garibaldi's departure until late in the evening. He was in such a hurry to join the General that he left his collar and his ink and pen on the table where he was writing a letter – relics preserved in the Republic's Museum. Aboard one of the boats driven ashore north of Magnavacca, he made his way to Comacchio where he unwisely took a room in the Albergo della Luna, believing himself to be safe even if caught by the Austrians on the grounds that he was not carrying arms. He was wrong. Hauled out of the inn, and put into chains, he was taken in an open cart to Bologna, where, with the connivance of the Church, he was imprisoned, tortured and hanged. Farini (by no means an ardent apologist for Garibaldi) wrote, 'Gorzkowski sent Bassi, the Barnabite monk, and Livraghi to the scaffold, drawn in a cart like assassins, without any form of trial, not even military, and without the consolation of the Viaticum, which Bassi earnestly entreated; the ecclesiastical power did not interfere, they died like Christians and brave men, and were buried like beasts, in a field. The people revered Bassi as a martyr, strewed garlands of flowers over the ground which covered his bones, and honour his memory to this day (1854).' One of the principal streets in Bologna is still named after him. But alas St James!

*　　*　　*

Ciceruacchio and his two sons, driven ashore on the same beach as Garibaldi, managed somehow to cross several of the mouths of the Po, trying desperately to reach Venice. But they were betrayed to the Austrians in the small town of San Nicolo, and shot in the main square. Towards the close of the tenth canto of his autobiographical poem, which tells of the Retreat, Garibaldi was to refer, bitter still, to the death of the younger son. He was only thirteen, and was said to have pleaded for the life of his father and brother.

Epilogue

Upon the sandy shore was shot and died
The lamb of those two boys. A rifle-bolt
Of one good soldier smithereened his skull.

*   *   *

Anita, near to death, was carried ashore by Garibaldi. There ensued terrible hours – days – of hide-and-seek in the marshes and lagoons of the Po delta. Not all the aid of a friend and local landowner, providentially arriving, could spare them continual changes of habitation: from one hut to another, disguised as peasants, they staggered, or were rowed and punted. At last, barely conscious, Anita was carried in a cart to a dairy-farm near Mandriole. Trevelyan describes it, 'It is a finely-built, spacious house, standing among vineyards; but the reeds and waste land of the southern marsh come almost to its doors, and from its upper chamber the tall trees of the famous pine-forest of Ravenna are seen, the nearest of them scarcely a mile away.'

Into this house she was borne, her husband and three other men each taking a corner of the mattress on which she lay. 'In putting it down on the bed,' Garibaldi wrote, 'I thought I saw the death-look in her face.' And so he had.

*   *   *

This was the nadir of Garibaldi's life. His most celebrated achievements still lay years ahead. At the moment he had no resources save an extraordinary stamina, even more extraordinary hope, and the companionship of one limping friend. This was Captain 'Leggiero', who had been wounded during the defence of Rome, and had managed to join the Retreat only in its later stages. The two of them hid for two days and nights in the pine-forests of Ravenna, and in a thatched hut nearby. Then they set off across Romagna and Tuscany, along an escape route organized by friends, to Cala Martina, just opposite the island of Elba. On September 2nd they embarked, and were taken to Genoa and Nice, where Garibaldi told his children, in the care of his parents, of the death of their mother. An embarrassment to the government of Piedmont, he left once again for exile, enjoying hospitality for a few winter months in Tangiers from both British and Piedmontese consuls, before going to America. He earned his living in a candle-factory in New York, became a ship's captain and travelled to Peru and to the China seas, and only in 1859 was able to return to Italy. The story of his recruitment of the Thousand, his sailing from Genoa to Sicily in two old steamers, his rolling-up of more than 20,000 Neapolitan troops on the island, his carrying the campaign across the straits of Messina and within weeks conquering Naples itself is the most heroic chapter of the Risorgimento: out of this great, irregular triumph was to be born the fact, and the fiction, of Italy One and Indivisible.

POSTFACE

THERE MAY BE READERS of this book who are as ignorant as I was, before setting out on my walk, of the role which Garibaldi played in the stormy years of the late 1840s. For them, I offer this potted guide: many excellent works in English, particularly those of Denis Mack Smith, and a recent biography of the General by Jasper Ridley are available for those who wish to pursue the subject.

The ideas of the French Revolution, Napoleon's conquest of Italy in the last decade of the eighteenth century, the subsequent reorganization of principalities and duchies, the reform of institutions of every sort – all those appalling disturbances were calmed, and the *status quo* more or less restored, by the work of the Congress of Vienna in 1815. Guided by Metternich, Austria became the effective overlord of most of northern and central Italy. Her rule was not, at least during the earlier years, a particularly oppressive one; although censorship was strict in those states such as Lombardy, which she governed directly, and conspiracy was snuffed out and savagely punished. Pellico's *Le mie prigioni* is a moving account of years spent in Spielberg prison.

One legacy of the heady Napoleonic days which it was impossible to eradicate was the idea of *Italy*. Not that this expressed itself in practical schemes for unity, so much as in the ever-growing desire to get rid of the foreigner, the Austrian. Secret societies flourished, uprisings and riots were fomented. In one of the abortive conspiracies in 1834, Garibaldi, then a sailor twenty-five years of age, was involved, and paid for it by enduring some fifteen years of exile in South America. Here he led an Italian legion in minor wars of liberation, fought with great hardihood on land and sea; and by the mid-'forties had become the romantic, legendary hero of Montevideo.

During this decade the pressures mounted for constitutional reform throughout Italy. With the granting of a constituent assembly the Kingdom of Piedmont became the most advanced of the states; and also gained ever greater freedom from Austrian influence. She began to build railways, encourage industry, modernize agriculture – and created the most efficient armed forces in Italy, under the aegis of the king, Charles Albert of the House of Savoy.

At the other extreme the Papal States (that ancient dominion dividing northern Italy from southern) was one of the most backward. The Holy See stood firm against change of every kind. To have built railways would have been to promote the work of the Devil. All administration remained in the hands of the clergy, all authority stemmed from the Pope. The temporal dominion was sacred.

The surprise election of Pius IX in 1846 was followed by his grant of amnesty to political prisoners. This created an explosion of joy far beyond his expectations. The new Pope was hailed as the Saviour of Italy, the Apostle of Freedom – and the enemy of Austria. He was at first delighted, then increasingly bewildered and alarmed, by the enthusiasm he everywhere aroused. Heretical England hailed him. The Sultan of Turkey sent him an embassy. Jews kissed the vestments of the long-awaited Messiah. Mazzini, despite his belief in 'God and the people' and his creed of revolutionary Republicanism, encouraged him to be strong in faith. Garibaldi wrote from Uruguay to offer him his sword. 'Now that we have a liberal pope,' complained Metternich, 'we can answer for nothing.'

Soon he was to find that the more reforms he granted, the more the people of Rome demanded of him. Elected assemblies, a civic guard, easing of censorship – where would it all end? He had once confessed that he did not understand the ABC of politics.

The answer was not long in coming. In March 1848, the revolution of Vienna toppled Metternich. Italy rose in tumult. The five days of the insurrection of Milan, the proclamation of the Republic of Venice, and the declaration of war against Austria by Piedmont followed within weeks.

For the Pope, this war posed a terrible dilemma. He was after all an Italian, and could not fail to be moved by the struggle for his country's independence. At first he temporized. He sent an army north, under his Piedmontese general, instructing it to defend the frontiers of the Papal States. He said, 'I have blessed the banner of our troops on condition they do not cross our borders' adding, with a sly smile, 'If they do cross, it will not be my fault.'

But this would not do. The contradiction between his duty as spiritual ruler of millions of Catholics throughout the world – including Austria – on the one hand, and as sovereign of an Italian state on the other, became too great for him. He continued to equivocate. But his popularity began to turn very sour. His subjects had asked for a crusade, and he gave them an Allocution.

Militarily, the failure of Rome wholeheartedly to support Piedmont made little difference. By August 9th Milan had been retaken by Marshal Radetzky, the Salasco armistice signed, and the first war of Italian independence been lost. Garibaldi, whose small army of 1500 or so irregulars was fighting for Lombardy, refused to surrender, and seized two paddle-steamers on Lake Maggiore. However, this was no more than a brave sideshow, and he was soon forced to flee into Switzerland.

That autumn and winter of '48, in the aftermath of defeat, were days, Farini said, 'in which mad discord brandished her torch over wretched Italy, in which Mazzini's Republicans heaped vituperation on the head of the worsted Charles Albert, and paraded everywhere the phantom of treachery with such glee that it seemed as if Radetzky's victory was the victory of their pride, their system and their party. They tried to induce Genoa to rise and also Leghorn; they inflamed the public mind against all kings and all governments, shouting 'the People', 'the People', 'Government by the people', 'War by the people' . . . etc. etc.

Rome, however, enjoyed a very brief period of relatively good fortune. The admirable Pellegrino Rossi, former French ambassador (though an Italian by birth), moderate, honest, a man of science and letters as well as of state, a sceptical observer of the frenzied demonstrations of the Roman mob, became in effect chief minister of the Pope. Plans for telegraph and railways were put in hand: interest on a Rothschild loan was even paid. There were attempts to form a Confederation of all the Italian States with the 'august and immortal Pontiff and his successors' as perpetual presidents. But nothing came of it. It was too late. Hated both by clericals of the right and by democrats of the left, Rossi was stabbed to death, almost certainly by the elder son of the Tribune of the

People Ciceruacchio, on the morning of November 15th, on the occasion of the opening of the Council of Deputies.

Ten days later, the Pope – who had been besieged by the mob in the Quirinal and seen one of his Prelates shot dead in the window of his chamber – fled at night, in disguise, to Gaeta in the Kingdom of Naples.

The revolution was now well under way, even although it was not until February 5th 1849 that a full and all-powerful assembly met – with Garibaldi present as Deputy from Macerata.* Then the Popedom was formally deposed from the Temporal Sovereignty, and a Republic declared: '. . . the form of Government shall be a pure democracy, and it shall receive the glorious appellation of the Republic of Rome.'

Meanwhile Pius IX had not been idle at Gaeta, though he scorned to treat with his usurpers. All his purpose lay in regaining his temporal dominions. They were his sacred trust. For would not the spiritual independence of the Papacy be lost, unless the Pope were sovereign in his own country? The faithful Catholic powers would surely come to his aid.

Nor were the Austrians slow to move. By February 18th they had entered Ferrara, and soon moved on Bologna. The Spaniards promised an expedition. His hosts the Bourbons said they would place their forces at his disposal. Piedmont was almost the only Catholic power whose aid was not solicited – her ambitions, territorial and democratic, were suspect.

The most eager of all to help was France. On the one hand, she would thereby please her Catholic constituency; to restore the Pope to his rightful seat was clearly the duty of the eldest daughter of the Church. But on the other hand, France was also the historic exporter of Liberty, the guardian of the ideals of the Revolution. The two roles might at first sight seem hard to reconcile; however, Louis Napoleon and his ministers succeeded in doing so. France would restore the Pope unaided – but only on condition that he promised to uphold the Constitution already granted his subjects, and to continue his reforms. In this way she would be preventing the thoroughly reactionary restoration inevitable if Austria performed the task. On a less ideological plane, her intervention would deny Austria suzerainty of the whole peninsula. And so, on April 24th 1849, a French division under General Oudinot

* Macerata near Ancona – not to be confused with the Macerata Feltria of the Retreat.

landed at Civita Vecchia, to 'come to the aid' of Rome.

By this time Mazzini had become effective leader of the Republican triumvirate. Piedmont's resumption of war against Austria, and her total defeat under the walls of Novara on March 23rd, considered together with the collapse of the Democratic revolution in Tuscany and the recall to the throne of the Grand Duke, meant that Mazzini could with some colour regard himself in Rome, and Manin in Venice, as the sole surviving champions of the ideal of Italian Unity and Freedom. Volunteers of all classes, from all parts of the country, rallied to Rome. The size of Garibaldi's irregular army, stationed at Rieti, grew and its discipline improved. When put to the test on April 30th at Castel Guido, against Oudinot's force of 6000 men – six times more numerous – victory was won after six hours' fierce fighting. Oudinot retired, shocked. He had thought Rome would open her gates to him, and had said 'Italians do not fight'.

The negotiations and the truce that followed gave Rome the opportunity to attend to the Neapolitan invaders. Ferdinand II by May 2nd had advanced as far as Albano, at the head of 12,000 men. First at Palestrina and then at Velletri he was routed by Garibaldi, and did not care to emerge again from his borders.

But the French could not be expected to accept the dishonour to their arms with such docility. Although De Lesseps (later to be more successful as the builder of the Suez Canal) arrived from Paris to negotiate a settlement whereby Rome would place herself under the protection of France, some 20,000 reinforcements were also hurried to Oudinot. The latter proved to be the more significant despatch, and when the terms of the treaty were repudiated and hostilities resumed – not without a likely element of bad faith – on June 3rd, there could be only one outcome. Yet a month still passed before Rome fell.

The epic tale of its defence – the old men, women and children gazing, as at Troy, from the battlements of Rome at the fight outside its gates, the lancer Masina spurring his horse four times up the steps of the Villa of the Four Winds before he was killed, Garibaldi riding everywhere on his white charger, accompanied by his Negro servant Aguyar – this is most stirringly told in Trevelyan's *Defence of the Roman Republic* (and at first hand by Hoffstetter, too); and forms the prelude to that long Retreat to that other Republic whose steps I retraced in the spring of 1980.

APPENDIX I

The Austrian View

AN ACCOUNT OF GARIBALDI'S MARCH was sent by Field-Marshal D'Aspre, Austrian C-in-C in Florence, to Marshal Van Martini and Count Esterhazy, who were respectively envoy at the Court of Naples and minister at the Holy See (then still at Gaeta).

It is interesting, if for no other reason, in that it tends to exculpate Major Muller, Garibaldi's cavalry commander, from treachery of which he was accused by Ruggieri (but not by Hoffstetter). Trevelyan repeats the charge. I am reluctant to believe that a Polish cavalry officer, whatever the cause he may serve, would ever betray his General. As will be seen, General Stadion is said to have *captured* his squad of 60 horse, who had lost their way.

The report also shows up the Austrian belief that Garibaldi was at first hoping to reach the western coast – an error which may be laid to the credit of his feints. The gross overestimate of his numbers would have pleased the General, too.

Here is what D'Aspre wrote:

'After Garibaldi had retired from Rome, and halted for a few days near Todi, which he had reached by several twists and turns, he suddenly broke out into Tuscany on July 18th at Cetona and Sarteano, occupying Montepulciano on the 19th. On receiving this news I immediately ordered Paumgartten's brigade, who previously had had orders to attack the rebels at Spoleto and Todi, to follow Garibaldi and attack him wherever he might come up to him.

'From here (Florence) Major-General Count Stadion was despatched to Siena with one battalion of infantry, one squadron of cavalry and three pieces of artillery.

'Various reports from spies led us to believe that Garibaldi intended to reach the Mediterranean through the Maremma, where some ships were already waiting for him. Our plan was to frustrate this attempt by General Stadion's marching from Siena to Orbetello via Buonconvento, Arcidosso and Scansano. In pursuance of this plan four companies were also transferred to Livorno, to take ship thence to Porto Santo Stefano.

'Meanwhile Garibaldi had left Montepulciano and proceeded to Montisi. But from there he suddenly changed direction towards Sinalunga, Foiano, Castiglion Fiorentino, and so to Arezzo. His force, which had at first been overestimated at 7–8000 men (including 800 horse) was reduced to 2500 men and 400 horse. His entire artillery consisted of one 3-pounder.

'This change of direction forced us to send from here another squadron of hussars and three cannons to Arezzo.

'General Stadion, who in the neighbourhood of Murlo had captured a squad of sixty horse who had lost their way, also made for Arezzo by the Buonconvento-Asciano road.

'The city, prompted by the Austrian commander of the hospital there, and emboldened by the presence of sixty of our convalescent soldiers, had taken the decision to deny Garibaldi entrance to the city, and had closed its gates. Provisions however were supplied.

'When on the 23rd the column of Paumgartten's brigade, which had continued to pursue the rebels from Montepulciano, arrived at Arezzo, and Garibaldi also heard of the arrival of the other two columns from Asciano and Montevarchi, he very quickly withdrew, desisting from attack. He fled by way of Anghiari, Citerna and Borgo San Sepolcro, once again crossed the borders of Tuscany, and camped near Mercatello. General Stadion directed one part of his troops to pursue him along this route, and another part towards Tebalda and Bagno, while General Paumgartten – and indeed Archduke Ernst too – were asked to advance from Perugia to Macerata,* and to proceed towards Urbino. General Count Gorzkowski was also asked to send troops from Bologna in the same direction.

'On the 25th we succeeded for the first time in catching up with the rearguard of the bold rebel condottiere in the neighbourhood of Monterchi. Some of his men were killed and some taken prisoner. On the same day we also seized a few of his horses near Anghiari.

'On the 28th the encirclement was carried out as planned and in the course of our advance, the vanguard of General Stadion's army and of Archduke Ernst's too engaged the enemy's rearguard,

* Not to be confused with Macerata Feltria, on Garibaldi's route.

which suffered considerable losses of men and horses, at Sant'Angelo in Vado.

'With his way to the sea blocked by Archduke Ernst, the enemy turned towards Macerata Feltria, across the mountains.

'On the evening of the 30th his advance guard arrived at San Marino. On the same day, near Carpegna, Garibaldi had made another attempt to break out into Tuscany, but three companies of Stadion's brigade, coming from Pennabilli, blocked this attempt. During the pursuit of July 31st troops of Archduke Ernst clashed once again with the enemy rearguard which, their nerves broken by previous engagements, fled precipitately, leaving behind their only cannon.

'On the 31st the entire territory of San Marino which Garibaldi had entered against the wishes of its Government, was surrounded. The gates were closed to him, but the government entered into negotiations.'

APPENDIX II

Garibaldi's Autobiographical Poem

Canto X   The Retreat

I HAVE ATTEMPTED TO RENDER into blank verse that part of
Garibaldi's long autobiographical poem which deals with the
Retreat from Rome..All I can claim is that it is not much worse than
the original. Its interest lies in its stark revelation of his attitudes, of
the firmness with which he cherished his beliefs, his loves and bitter
enmities – if you like, of his simple-mindedness. It was written late
in his life and is, as will be seen, addressed to himself, as the Outcast.

> Outcast, go forward on your path! A clutch
> You'll always find of those who scorn to bear
> The weight of chains. In vain four Kings send bands
> Of hirelings in pursuit. The Holy Grail
> You carry in your heart for Italy
> Will not this time be broken. No – you're saved
> For arduous tasks to come. You'll still disturb
> The sleep of spies of state. Your Bay's iron shoe
> Seen stamped in Royal palaces, will teach
> The insolent their hour is near, they too
> Must taste the bread of tragedy, the hurt.
> How dull is made the crowd! The priest sows lies,
> Alludes to God's chastisement, and applause
> Breaks out amongst the multitude, against
> The Few who hate the Tyrant. Duller still
> The mercenary affront th' Italian troop
> Who's resolute! The lion who's pressed upon
> By hordes of jackals sometimes halts, and turns,
> So that the craven mob upon his heels
> Shrinks back in fright to see him unafraid.
> Thus hireling crews, puffed bold by numbers, bid
> To attack the honoured remnant, sacred core

Of Italy. But what reins back the gangs'
Bravado? Tumbling heights of Apennines,
The warrior mien of my own band of men!
Then safe at last the neutral plot is reached
Of San Marino, sole land unenslaved
Of Italy, whose people welcomed us
Most kind, as brothers, soldiers come back home,
Yet what? Does overweening Force respect
The shrine devoted to neutrality?
Laws, Justice, vaunted Human Rights – to Force
Mere empty words! The Big Battalion's Law,
The Tyrant's whim is Justice. Ever thus
It will be while the slave swears faith
And service to th' impostors: while the soul
Comes second to the stomach. Soul? Do sots,
Do lukewarm men, do Moderates, have *souls*?
Italians! Tire not when the time returns
For you once more to wield the patriot's sword!
That deadly beast that's stamped you underfoot
For generations – let it pay the fee
Of its vile crimes! And while this paradise
Of ours on earth still harbours one – yes one –
Accursed foreign foe, sheath not your sword!
That wicked breed who want what is not theirs
Like couch-grass spreads its tentacles beneath
Our soil. And yet how often have I seen
You tire upon the holy stage of War
And let the fields grow rank with weeds when weeds'
Uprooting would not tax you! Glorious
To finish once for all the ransom-task!
One band of heroes now forever holds
The banner of Italian Courage high,
Forever is prepared for harder proofs
Where'er the fight for Liberty is fought.
Yet too uncaring, too inconstant are
The masses: thus it is the Few who fall
And with them falls in shameful servitude
Our Italy!
'Now to your hearth and home, my weary band
Of young companions in arms, return!

Yet do not tell your wife you tired, and left
Our Italy in foreign thrall, but say
To her that you were bid farewell, and swore
To save your country from its servitude
So soon as you to service were called back.'
And meanwhile see me following, who am
Cast out, rejected from this land I deeply love,
And with me see my wife, inseparable
Companion of the Outcast, fearless . . . Ah,
So sick, unfortunate! She never more
Will see her darling babies! On the sands,
The shifting, empty sands of Adria
Her miseries will end. No stone, no cross
Will signal to the passer-by the bones
Of one who dies for Italy, who oft
Urged on her warriors to free our land.
Oh woman of my heart! How hard it was
To give this sacrifice to Italy!
And ah! the burden nurtured in your womb!
Yet thanks to weak hermaphrodites, your dear
Surviving babes may one day need to cast
Themselves into war's furnace, too – the fight
For Italy's great soul not ended yet.
Meanwhile the coward guzzles, boasting loud
Of Triumphs not his own, dishonouring
In his mean blood the people's name and pride.

'Dismount! Disarm those felons!' so I cried
To my companions, that day we came
To Cesenatico! And in a flash
The few spy-lackeys serving Austria
Those blots and burdens on our native land
Were taken and disarmed. Fine prelude, this,
To our salvation since thereon we seized
A dozen boats, and we might well have reached
The city of lagoons. But Fortune still
Refused her smile. For then a tempest rose
And lashed the waves of Adria. They foamed
And crashed and broke whitehorsed. To hunted men
They barred the way from out the narrow mouth

Of Cesenatico. The warping-chains
Unbroken yet, tugged back the fishing-boats
Towards the lap of those high waves, tugged back
My dangered band of men toward the swarm
Of Austrians fast approaching. Had the core
Of my surviving faithful thus been kept
For one more slaughter? No – at last I sailed
Out with my few. Together on one boat
Were joined with me my wife, in grievous pain,
My Bassi, and brave Ciceruacchio,
That noblest tribune of the Roman plebs,
And his two much-beloved beardless boys.
In silence then I fixed my gaze upon
Those dear ones. Ah! and to my consort stretched
A hand to give a sip of water, last
Small wretched comfort to an ebbing life.
It was a sunset, such as seen in days
More fortunate. My heart embittered then
By present grief, I sadly turned my eyes
And looked on Nature's first and fairest son,
The Son whom in my early years I used
In joy and reverence to greet, upon
His rising and his falling in the waves.
And now, 'That thus' I cried out loud, 'thou shouldst
See fit to mark the last sad evening hour
Of this most piteous life – that is no life!'
And thou, who dost console the grieving ones,
Propitiator Goddess of the Night
Whose milky orb so oft doth rise to bring
To those who sail in peril on the sea
Sweet comfort – guidance to the voyager
Who's lost in desert wastes! Thou enemy
This night! Informer to a tyrant's gang!
To hunters didst thy brilliance betray
The boats that ferried luckless ones in flight!
And then as mastiffs on our trail, the fleet
All crowded on. How easy their assault
And scattering of those miserable Few
Who yet flew high the flag of War, though torn
And riddled! Yes, the flag which Italy

Could yet be proud of, yet display!
Our thirteen boats were scattered wide. Few beached.
The Austrians took captive most of us.
Ashore I struggled with my burden dear,
Dear dying burden! Heartbroken – none
Can tell my grief. But on they pressed, those boats
Which hounded us, those crowds upon the beach
Of Austrians, those priest-policemen too –
A noisy pack, who sniffed their prey like dogs.
Enveloped in a mist we must have been,
As in the days of old. I laid her down
A little distance from the shore, to guard
My treasured one, and never had I loved
So much, the mother of my darling babes.
And who should fall into th' assassins' nails
Not far from here but Bassi, Christ's true priest?
A savage, savage death he was to face –
The wicked crew of Ministers of Hell
Fine torture for him first desired. Nearby
Fell Ciceruacchio, with both his sons.
Upon the sandy shore was shot and died
The lamb of those two boys. A rifle-butt
Of one good soldier smithereened his skull.

And nowadays the Moderates spare nought
To win as friends the Austrians we fought!

BIBLIOGRAPHY

In the great bibliography of Garibaldi compiled by Antony Campanella in 1971 no fewer than 380 entries refer to the Retreat from Rome, and the flight from Comacchio to Cala Martina. I have consulted, even if briefly, very many of these, and so will confine myself here to listing the works of which I have made the most extensive use.

BELLUZZI, Raffaele; *La Ritirata di Garibaldi*, Bologna 1887
BESEGHI, Umberto; *Ugo Bassi*, Parma 1939
BRIZI, Oreste; *Le bande garibaldine a San Marino*, Arezzo 1850
CORSI, Carlo; *Venticinque anni in Italia*, Firenze 1870
FARINI, Luigi; *The Roman State*, London 1851
FORBES, Hugh; *Manual for the Patriotic Volunteer*, New York 1855
GARIBALDI, Gius.; *Poema Autobiografico*, Bologna 1911
HOFFSTETTER, G. de; *Giornale delle cose di Roma*, Torino 1851
MAGHERINI-GRAZIANI, Giov; *Aneddoti . . . sul passaggio di G.G. per l'alta valle del Tevere*, Città di Castello 1896
MASI, Ernesto; *Il risorgimento Italiano*, Firenze 1917
RIDLEY, Jasper; *Garibaldi*, London 1964
RUGGIERI, E.; *Della Ritirata di Garibaldi*, Genoa 1850
SANBORN, Franklin; *Life and Letters of John Brown* [for information on Forbes], Boston 1885
TREVELYAN, G. M.; *Garibaldi's Defence of the Roman Republic*, London 1907
State Archives for 1849 at Terni, Orvieto, Cetona, Sarteano, Torrita, Castiglion Fiorentino, Arezzo, San Sepolcro, Città di Castello, Sant'Angelo in Vado, Urbania, Urbino, Macerata Feltria
Diocesan Archives at Città di Castello

INDEX

I have chosen not to enter Garibaldi, who appears *passim* in these pages, except where light is cast on his character and aims. Similarly with the admirable Major Hoffstetter, whose liking for food and wine, and splendid views, seemed worth indexing. I have omitted those people and places which are very marginal to my tale – and those which form the subject of whole chapters, too.

Places in Italics, people in Roman.

Index